This new critical study of Ibsen's ... mental questions of text, reception ... performance. What is the definitive 'version' of *A Doll's House*: original text, translation, stage presentation, radio version, adaptation to film or television? What occurs when a drama intended for recipients in one language is translated into another, or when a play written for the stage is adapted for radio, television or film? And to what extent do differences between the media and between directorial approaches influence the meaning of the play text? Discussions of these issues include an internal analysis of the dramatic text and comparative performance analysis, framed by the biographical background to the play and its impact on dramas by Strindberg, Shaw and O'Neill and on films by Ingmar Bergman. The book concludes with a list of productions and a select bibliography.

IBSEN

A Doll's House

PLAYS IN PRODUCTION

Series editor: Michael Robinson

PUBLISHED VOLUMES

Ibsen: *A Doll's House* by Egil Törnqvist
Miller: *Death of a Salesman* by Brenda Murphy
Molière: *Don Juan* by David Whitton

IBSEN

A DOLL'S HOUSE

EGIL TÖRNQVIST

University of Amsterdam

Published by the Press Syndicate of the University of Cambridge
The Pitt Building, Trumpington Street, Cambridge CB2 1RP
40 West 20th Street, New York, NY 10011–4211, USA
10 Stamford Road, Oakleigh, Melbourne 3166, Australia

© Cambridge University Press 1995

First published 1995, 1998

Printed in the United Kingdom at the University Press, Cambridge

A catalogue record for this book is available from the British Library

Library of Congress cataloguing in publication data applied for

ISBN 0 521 43386X hardback
ISBN 0 521 478669 paperback

CONTENTS

ILLUSTRATIONS

GENERAL PREFACE

Volumes in the series Plays in Production will take major dramatic texts and examine their transposition, firstly onto the stage and, secondly, where appropriate, into other media. Each book will include concise but informed studies of individual dramatic texts, focusing on the original theatrical and historical context of a play in relation to its initial performance and reception followed by subsequent major interpretations on stage, both under the impact of changing social, political and cultural values, and in response to developments in the theatre generally.

Many of the plays will also have been transposed into other media – film, opera, television, ballet – which may well be the form in which they are first encountered by a contemporary audience. Thus, a substantial study of the play text and the issues it raises for theatrical realisation will be supplemented by an assessment of such adaptations as well as the production history, where the emphasis will be on the development of a performance tradition for each work, including staging and acting styles, rather than simply the archaeological reconstruction of past performances.

Plays included in the series are all likely to receive regular performance and individual volumes will be of interest to the informed reader as well as to students of theatre history and literature. Each book also contains an annotated production chronology as well as numerous photographs from key performances.

Michael Robinson
University of East Anglia

PREFACE

Since its publication over a hundred years ago Ibsen's *A Doll's House*, now generally recognised as one of the milestones in world drama, has received much attention both in the theatre, in the living-room and in the classroom. Still frequently and widely performed, there are several reasons for the play's continuing popularity. Its central theme of self-realisation is neither time- nor space-bound. Its forceful illumination of woman's position in society makes it especially relevant in periods and countries where this issue is particularly burning. Moreover, the play is exceedingly well constructed. And it contains one of the most relished female roles in world drama.

Although there is by now a comprehensive literature about *A Doll's House*, most of it deals with the play as a text for readers. Much less has been said about it as a 'text' for spectators. And yet we may assume that it was this last category of recipients that Ibsen originally had in mind.

In the present book it is this latter 'text', the performance text, that is central. How has it been fashioned by leading directors? How has it been presented in various media? How do older productions relate to more recent ones? And how do those in Ibsen's native Scandinavia – with the strong linguistic and cultural ties that exist between the Nordic countries – relate to those outside this part of the world? These are the questions that will be discussed in the present study.

In the following, I quote from Ibsen's Norwegian original – as reproduced in *Samlede Verker: Hundreårsutgave* (Collected Works: Centenary Edition) – only when this is necessary, in which case I also provide an English translation. Normally I quote from the translation most frequently used in British productions, that by Michael Meyer. When this does not seem wholly adequate for my purpose, I resort to a variant of my own.

There is some variation in the typography of the different textual versions of *A Doll's House*. Since such variation seems both irrelevant and disturbing, I have deemed it wise to standardise the typography as follows:

(1)   For stage- and acting-directions in the source and target texts I use italics throughout and surround them by parentheses. By contrast, there are no parentheses surrounding stage- and acting-directions in adaptations of the text and in my transcriptions of performance passages.

(2)   Figure designations inside stage- and acting-directions as well as cue designations are capitalised and printed in roman.

References to *A Doll's House* are to 'sequences' rather than pages, since page numbers would vary with almost every edition of the play, whereas sequences, once agreed upon, remain constant. Further information about the sequence reference system is found on pp. 20–1. An integral sequence scheme of the play appears on pp. 169–72.

A remark must be made on the use of tense with regard to the various formats of *A Doll's House* discussed in this book. The principle followed is that for durative (repeatable) presentational modes the present tense is used, whereas the past tense is used for non-durative modes. Thus Nora 'enters' in the play text (as well as in translations of it) and in radio, television and film versions of it, whereas she 'entered' in stage presentations. The incidental presence nowadays of durative recordings also of the last-mentioned category – in the form of records and (video) tapes – cannot change the fundamental fact that the intended situation of reception has been that of a live performance, that is, a non-repeatable theatrical event.

Titles of non-English works are given in English translation; the original titles are added in the index.

ACKNOWLEDGEMENTS

While working on this book, I have had ample opportunity for discussing aspects of it with teachers and students at various universities. This has meant refreshing escapes from the isolated existence of individual research. I am very grateful to scenographer Gunilla Palmstierna-Weiss for her generous information concerning the two *Doll's House* productions, directed by Ingmar Bergman, for which she made the stage design and the costumes. I am also indebted to Dr Tom Olsson, former librarian of the Royal Dramatic Theatre in Stockholm, for enabling me to check my own impressions in the theatre against a video registration of Bergman's 1989 production, as well as to Eva Block of the National Archive of Recorded Sound and Moving Images in Stockholm for helping me to some of the audiovisual material. I am especially grateful to the Board of the recently opened Centre for Ibsen Studies in Oslo for enabling me, as a guest scholar in the autumn of 1993, to profit from the services of the Centre and of the University Library.

Parts of the book have earlier appeared in the following publications:
Transposing Drama: Studies in Representation, London: Macmillan, 1991, pp. 62–94;
'Ingmar Bergman's *Doll's Houses*', *Scandinavica*, Vol. 30, No. 1, May 1991, pp. 63–76;
'Ibsen ur teatersemiotisk synvinkel: Kring slutet i *Et dukkehjem*', *Studia Germanica Gandensia*, 28, and *Tijdschrift voor Skandinavistiek*, Vol. 12, Nos. 1–2, 1991, pp. 111–18;
'Comparative Performance Semiotics: The End of Ibsen's *A Doll's*

House', *Theatre Research International*, Vol. 19, No. 2, 1994, pp. 156–64.

I gratefully acknowledge permission to reprint the articles in *Scandinavica* and *Theatre Research International*.

CHAPTER 1
PROLOGUE: BACKGROUND

'There are two kinds of moral law, two kinds of conscience, one in man and a completely different one in woman. They do not understand each other; but in matters of practical living the woman is judged by man's law, as if she were not a woman but a man.'[1]

With these words Henrik Ibsen (1828–1906) in 1878 began the notes for what was to become one of the first truly realistic plays in world drama.[2] He called it *Et Dukkehjem*, a title which has traditionally been rendered in English as *A Doll's House*. Although this rendering has recently been questioned, I shall adhere to the traditional title; the reasons for this will be given later.

It is a remarkable fact that 'the father of modern drama' was born and bred in one of the outskirts of Europe, far away from cultural centres and theatres of any significant standing. Born in the small town of Skien in southern Norway, Ibsen was the second son in a family of six children. His father, Knud Ibsen, for some time a wealthy merchant, lost nearly everything he possessed when Henrik was only seven. Socially humiliated, the family had to move out of town to a small country house, Venstøp. Having left school in 1843, Ibsen the year after became an apothecary's assistant in the small coastal town of Grimstad. During his seven years there he wrote his first poems and his first play, *Catiline*, published under the pseudonym of Brynjolf Bjarme in 1850. He also fathered his first – illegitimate – son, by one of the maids. When he left Grimstad for Christiania, the capital later renamed Oslo, his intention was to study at the university. Although he failed in this, he was successful in having his second play, *The Warrior's Barrow*, staged by the

Danish-oriented Christiania Theatre in 1850. His literary talents were soon recognised by the virtuoso violinist Ole Bull who offered Ibsen a job as a stage manager and director at the National Theatre he had just founded in Bergen. Here Ibsen remained between 1851 and 1857, writing five plays, some of which he staged. In Bergen he became thoroughly familiar both with contemporary drama, notably the so-called well-made play, and with the problems involved in mounting plays for the stage. Having learnt the theatrical trade, he was in 1857 appointed artistic director of the Norwegian Theatre in Christiania. The year after he married Suzannah Thoresen, who bore him a son, Sigurd. Seeing his plans for an ambitious repertoire thwarted, Ibsen gradually began to neglect his work. When the theatre in 1862 went bankrupt, he had to resign. Along with his wife and their little son he left his native country in 1864, utterly disappointed in Norwegian politics, not to return to it permanently until 1891. Most of his twenty-seven years of voluntary exile were spent in Italy and Germany. Back in Norway, he wrote his last four plays. In 1900 he suffered a stroke which left him unable to do any futher writing until his death six years later.

When Ibsen composed *A Doll's House* he had already published fourteen plays, many of which are historical dramas. His breakthrough came with the masterly verse drama *Brand* (1865), two years later followed by the equally impressive *Peer Gynt*. Ibsen's inclination to compose his plays dialectically is already here fully apparent. After the idealist extremist Brand the compromising materialist Peer Gynt followed logically – just as later Nora in *A Doll's House*, who breaks up from an unsatisfactory marriage, was to be succeeded by Mrs Alving in *Ghosts*, who remains in such a marriage. As Ibsen succinctly put it: 'after Nora, Mrs Alving of necessity had to come'.[3]

The plot of *A Doll's House*, centred around the discovery of Nora's forgery, was based on an event in real life. In 1870 Laura Kieler (*née* Petersen) had sent Ibsen a sequel to *Brand*, which she called *Brand's Daughters*. The year after they met. Ibsen took an interest in the young, pretty and vivacious girl. He invited her to Dresden and for two months in the summer of 1872 'the lark', as he liked to call her, visited his home almost daily. A couple of years later she married. After a while, the husband fell ill. The doctor advised a long vacation in a warm climate, and Laura secretly borrowed money to finance the trip. In 1876 they set off for Switzerland and Italy. On their way home they stopped briefly in Munich, where Laura in confidence told Suzannah about the debt she had made for the trip and which she had kept secret. Ibsen later urged her to tell her husband about it so that he could help her. Afraid to do so, she tried instead to get the payment postponed. When this failed, she falsified a note.

> The forgery was discovered, and the bank refused payment; whereupon she told her husband the whole story. He, regardless of the fact that she had done it purely for his sake … told her she was unworthy to have charge of their children and … had her committed to a public asylum … and demanded a separation so that the children could be removed from her care. After a month she was discharged from the asylum and, for the children's sake, begged her husband to take her back, which he very grudgingly agreed to do.[4]

Although Nora's situation in *A Doll's House* is similar to Laura's, Ibsen reversed it when he had the wife divorce her husband rather than the other way around. He also deviated from the real-life model by refraining from a return on Nora's part.

The central theme of *A Doll's House* can be traced back to several of Ibsen's earlier plays. In *Brand* Agnes leaves Ejnar after discovering that he lacks the courage and strength to risk his life for another's salvation.[5] Her Kierkegaardian ethics and her disillusioning discovery correspond to Nora's.

The doll motif is anticipated in *The League of Youth* (1869), where Ibsen depicts a kindred spirit to Nora in

> Selma, 'the fairytale princess,' longing for the true fairytale, always kept on the outside and never permitted to make her contribution in the struggles of real life. She must always be protected from all that is

ugly. Finally she cries out in anger: 'You dressed me like a doll; you played with me, as one plays with a child. I would have rejoiced to bear a burden; I longed with all my heart for everything that storms, that lifts up, exalts.'[6]

Again, in *Pillars of Society* (1877) Ibsen points to the discrimination against women. In one of the early drafts of this play Consul Bernick says: 'We don't notice women.' In the final version these words are handed over to Lona Hessel who, anticipating Nora, turns them against the men: 'You don't notice women.' Like Lona Hessel, Dina Dorf defies society and refuses to bow to 'all these intimidating considerations ... all this killing respectability'. In the first draft Ibsen went even further. Here Dina Dorf 'is willing to enter into an unconsecrated union with the man she loves; she would throw off all external bonds, even this hated thing of "betrothal", in order to be free, herself alone'.[7]

It was presumably after becoming acquainted with the Norwegian feminist writer Camilla Collett in 1871 that Ibsen became deeply concerned with questions pertaining to man–woman relations in contemporary society. Along with the decline of barter economy and the concomitant growth of industrialisation, the social position of women – especially women of the middle class – had become undermined. As mass-produced commodities had come to replace home-made ones, the division of labour between men and women, husbands and wives, characteristic of agrarian society, was replaced by a system where the husband, away from home, became the sole breadwinner, while at home the housekeeping was done largely by servants. (In *A Doll's House* there are significantly two maids caring for the Helmer household.) Prevented from higher education and from attractive social posts, the roles of married women were reduced to those of mother and sexual partner.

It was only natural that a number of writers should react against this state of things. In Sweden Carl Jonas Love Almqvist and Fredrika Bremer had been remarkable forerunners of the emancipation movement already in the 1830s. Camilla Collett, responsible for the first Norwegian problem novel, made her contribution to it in the 1850s. But it was not until the 1870s that there was a more general demand for emancipatory reforms. There can be little doubt that many of the fictional works dealing with man–woman relations, of marriage as a social institution, and so on, not only gave rise to a lively debate but actually helped to push these reforms. John Stuart Mill's *The Subjection of Women* (1869) was immediately published in Danish, in a translation by Georg Brandes. Although Mill pleaded for equal rights between the sexes, he held the opinion that married women should be housewives and mothers.

As the leading critic in Scandinavia at the time, Brandes was very influential and his radical standpoint in the woman question, combined with his insistence that literature should above all debate current problems, had a strong impact on Scandinavian writers. If Brandes' *Main Currents in 19th Century Literature* (1872–90) may be said to have launched the first wave of discussion around these questions in the 1870s, Ibsen's *A Doll's House* and *Ghosts* (1881) initiated the second and much more extensive debate in the 1880s, a debate, centering on sexual morals, which at that time could hardly have taken place anywhere else.[8]

Ibsen's attitude to the women's rights movement has been a matter of some dispute.[9] While many critics – mostly feminists – have been inclined to see the playwright as a fervent proponent of improved *women's* rights, others have found him more concerned with *human* rights.

Adherents of the first opinion will point not only to the preliminary notes for the play but also to the fact that Ibsen in January 1879

> proposed to the Scandinavian Society that a woman librarian be hired. As a second measure he recommended that women be given the right to vote in the society ... He insisted that the present situation was a 'humiliation' to women who, he insisted, possessed along with young people and the true artist, 'the instinct of genius that unconsciously hits upon the truth'.[10]

Adherents of the second opinion will quote from Ibsen's speech at the banquet offered in his honour by the Norwegian Society for Women's Rights on 26 May 1898. On this occasion he declared:

> I have been more of a poet and less of a social philosopher than people generally tend to suppose. ... I must disclaim the honour of having consciously worked for women's rights. I am not even quite sure what women's rights really are. To me it has been a question of human rights. And if you read my works carefully you will realise that. Of course it is incidentally desirable to solve the problem of women [*sic*]; but that has not been my whole object. My task has been the portrayal of human beings.[11]

How valid is this statement made twenty years after *A Doll's House* was composed, in a period when Ibsen was little concerned with social problems? Not very, those would say who regard Ibsen as a playwright developing away from timely questions in the early social plays to more individual and universal problems in the late ones. Extremely relevant, those would claim who see a fundamental unity in his work, centred around more or less timeless ethical problems. Close examination of Ibsen's polyinterpretable play text has brought no definite solution to the problem. While one critic rejects male chauvinist attempts to 'save Ibsen from feminism',[12] another, comparing the first complete draft with the published version, suggests that the playwright while working on the play actually made Nora less feminine and more human.[13]

As Ibsen himself indicates in his speech, the distinction between 'women's rights' and 'human rights' seems somewhat academic. The two concepts were certainly exceedingly intertwined when he wrote *A Doll's House* – as Nora's conviction that she is 'first and foremost a human being' indicates, the connotation being that as a woman she fights for human rights. The distinction is nevertheless important when applied to the play, since the former concept suggests that *A Doll's House* is a problem drama, while the latter indicates that it is a tragedy.

The genesis of *A Doll's House* can be traced mainly thanks to Ibsen's letters to his Copenhagen publisher, Frederik Hegel. Thus in a letter of 5 May 1878 he informs the publisher of a new 'drama of modern life' in four acts. As far as we know, this is the first reference to what was later to become *A Doll's House*.

In his highly interesting 'Notes for the Tragedy of Modern Times', dated Rome 19 October 1878, Ibsen gives a brief outline of the theme of the new play. After the initial paragraph, quoted at the beginning of this chapter, the notes continue:

> The wife in the play ends up quite bewildered and not knowing right from wrong; her natural instincts on the one side and her faith in authority on the other leave her completely confused.
>
> A woman cannot be herself in contemporary society, it is an exclusively male society with laws drafted by men, and with counsel and judges who judge feminine conduct from the male point of view.
>
> She has committed a crime, and she is proud of it; because she did it for love of her husband and to save his life. But the husband, with his conventional views of honour, stands on the side of the law and looks at the affair with male eyes.
>
> Mental conflict. Depressed and confused by her faith in authority, she loses faith in her moral right and ability to bring up her children. Bitterness. A mother in contemporary society, just as certain insects go away and die when she has done her duty in the propagation of the race [*sic*]. Love of life, of home and husband and children and family. Now and then, woman-like, she shrugs off her thoughts. Sudden return of dread and terror. Everything must be borne alone. The catastrophe approaches, ineluctably, inevitably. Despair, resistance, defeat.[14]

What Ibsen had in mind, judging by these notes, was a play in which an ethical problem was related to a contemporary social situation. The protagonist of the intended play is 'a woman' and 'a mother', that is, a representative of all women, all mothers. What

Ibsen wished to describe was not an individual situation, not even a typical one but an archetypal one. This explains why he called the planned drama 'the Tragedy of Modern Times'.

What the notes are concerned with is how feminine instinct (nature) is pitted against masculine regulative thinking (culture). The ethics of the suppressed female are opposed to those of the suppressing male. Male sense of identity is contrasted with female lack of the same. And the implication seems to be that once male society is abolished, a better society will arise, characterised by equality between the sexes and, as a result of this, more natural and human ethics.

Four months after the preliminary notes had been penned, on 18 February 1879, Ibsen writes the publisher that he is completely engrossed in the new work. While working on the play,

> Ibsen was nervous and retiring and lived in a world alone, which gradually became peopled with his own imaginary characters. Once he suddenly remarked to his wife: 'Now I have seen Nora. She came right up to me and put her hand on my shoulder.' 'How was she dressed?' asked his wife. 'She had a simple blue cotton dress,' he replied without hesitation.[15]

Similarly, Ibsen's daughter-in-law has recalled how the playwright, while working on *A Doll's House*, could experience Nora as a real person whom he expected to meet.[16]

On 22 May 1879 Ibsen could inform Hegel that much of the playwriting had been done: 'The new work deals with modern life and is of a predominantly serious character. It is in three long acts … I still want to think a little more about the title …'[17] By this time he had almost finished the final draft version of the first act, dated 2–24 May.

On 19 June, midway through the second act, Ibsen warned Hegel that the play might be somewhat delayed: 'in order to give the language and the dialogue generally the greatest possible perfection of form, I propose to write it out once more with improvements, corrections and alterations before I eventually send you the final fair-copy'.[18]

The play was completed in Amalfi, where Ibsen had moved for the summer months. In mid-September it was sent off, in three instalments, to the publisher, one of them accompanied by the playwright's remark: 'So much is certain: I cannot remember any of my other books giving me greater satisfaction than this one whilst working out the details of it.'[19]

A comparison between the first complete draft and the published version reveals that Ibsen's 'improvements' concerned much significant stage business, such as Nora's eating of macaroons, her poking the stove, her offering Rank a light for his cigar, her practising the tarantella and her changing into everyday clothes at the end. Not until the final version does the Christmas tree become symbolically pregnant or does Ibsen manipulate the lighting.[20] Another striking change which no longer may seem an improvement, is that Helmer was turned into a narrow-minded male chauvinist.[21]

A Doll's House was published in Copenhagen on 4 December 1879 in an edition of 8,000 copies, an exceedingly large number for a Scandinavian play even today. This edition was sold out within two weeks. A second and third edition were brought out within three months.

Seventeen days after its publication, on 21 December, the play had its successful world première at the Royal Theatre in Copenhagen. Ibsen, who rarely went to see his own plays, did not attend it. But when the first unbowdlerised German production of the play was launched in Munich on 3 March 1880, he was among the audience. The Norwegian novelist John Paulsen, who accompanied him, has recorded his reactions:

> Ibsen had attended several rehearsals; the play was, to Paulsen's mind, well acted, and went down excellently with the public. After the premiere, Ibsen thanked everyone who had taken part in the production warmly. But afterwards, at home, he was full of criticism,

not merely of the interpretation of the play and the various roles, but of details such as that Nora had the wrong-sized hands ... and that the colour of the wallpaper in the Helmers' apartment was wrong and conveyed a false atmosphere.[22]

Withholding publicly his dissatisfaction with the performance, Ibsen apparently held the opinion that a playwright should not meddle with productions of his own plays. His work is finished when he hands his text over to the publisher. What he *can* do – and what Ibsen is doing to a much greater extent than earlier playwrights – is to 'direct' his own plays by providing them with ample stage- and acting-directions. In the following chapter, dealing with the drama text, we shall see how this is done.

CHAPTER 2

THE DRAMA TEXT

Before examining the text of *A Doll's House*, it may be helpful to provide the reader with a synopsis of the play:

Act I. Christmas Eve. The Helmers' living-room. Nora Helmer returns home from a shopping-trip, loaded with Christmas gifts for her three children and for her husband Torvald, who has just been appointed manager of the Credit Bank with a substantial increase in salary. Mrs Linde, an old friend whom Nora has not seen for ten years, makes a surprise call. Nora reveals a secret to her. When she and Helmer were first married, Helmer had a serious illness and was forced to live for a time in Italy. To pay for this, Nora secretly borrowed a sum secured on the signature of her now dead father. Since that time she has been repaying the loan with whatever she has been able to save.

As soon as Helmer appears, Nora persuades him to provide a job at the bank for Mrs Linde. Nils Krogstad, a bank employee of dubious reputation, calls on Helmer. It is from Krogstad that Nora has borrowed the money. Left alone with her, Krogstad demands to know whether he is to be replaced in the bank by Mrs Linde. (Years ago the two had an affair.) He threatens that, should he be discharged, he will not only reveal Nora's secret to her husband but also disclose that she forged her dead father's signature. When Helmer returns, he declares Krogstad a cunning forger and lectures Nora on the dangerous influence he could exert.

Act II. Christmas Day. The same room. Nora awaits Krogstad's letter to her husband. She is saddened when Helmer again refuses to spare Krogstad and she resolves to ask Dr Rank, a close friend of the Helmers, for money to redeem her note. But before she has the opportunity to do so, Rank reveals that he is soon to die of an inherited disease. He also reveals that he has been in love with her for many years. These revelations make Nora feel that she cannot ask Rank for help.

Krogstad returns secretly, to tell her that he has prepared a letter informing her husband of the loan. Nora hints that she is contemplating suicide. As he leaves, Krogstad drops the letter in the letter-box.

Mrs Linde, who is now fully informed, leaves to visit Krogstad in order to plead for Nora. Meanwhile Nora rehearses the tarantella she is to perform at a fancy-dress ball the following evening.

Act III. Boxing Day. The same room. While the Helmers are at the fancy-dress ball upstairs, Mrs Linde and Krogstad meet in their living-room. There is a reconciliation between the former lovers, now both widowed and in need of each other. Mrs Linde's faith in Krogstad reawakens the goodness in him. He wants to withdraw the letter, but Mrs Linde feels that Nora must tell her husband the truth.

Back from the party, Helmer, excited by the champagne and by Nora's dancing, claims his 'conjugal rights'. Rank interrupts them. As he leaves, a black-crossed card dropped into the letter-box confirms Nora's suspicion that Rank's 'good night' is in fact a final leave-taking.

When Rank has left, Helmer opens the letter-box. Having read Krogstad's letter, he begins to scold his wife violently for causing such a blow to ethics and to his social position. They must continue with the pretence of married life, he states, but Nora will no longer be allowed to bring up her children. When a second letter from Krogstad arrives, saying that, in remorse, he is destroying the bond, Helmer is relieved. But Nora compels him to sit down for their first serious talk in the eight years they have been married.

She tells him that, having lived first as her father's 'doll child', then as Helmer's 'doll wife', she must now try to educate herself. Moreover, after Helmer's revealing reaction to the two letters, she has discovered that she has been living all these years with 'a stranger'. She leaves the house, telling her husband that reconciliation can come only if their 'life together' could become a true marriage. Helmer, left alone, clings to this idea.

Reduced to its essence, the plot of *A Doll's House* may be sketched as follows. In Act I, the major question we ask ourselves is: Will Nora's forgery be revealed? Already here it is apparent that Krogstad (the antagonist) is a threat to her. Act II deals with Nora's attempts to find an escape from this threatening situation. She first tries to persuade Helmer to let Krogstad stay in the bank. When this fails, she contemplates borrowing money from Rank but his declaration of love after his announcement of his imminent death make this impossible. She finally tries to prevent Krogstad from disclosing anything, this too in vain. Having failed in all her attempts, Nora in the final act realises that her forgery *will* be known. We now ask ourselves: How will Helmer react to this? The crisis comes as Helmer reads Krogstad's first letter, in which he threatens to reveal the forgery. Helmer, fearing a public scandal, at this point violently attacks Nora. But when he reads Krogstad's second letter, in which the threat is withdrawn, he forgives her (peripety). Helmer's true nature now stands clear to Nora. Far from being the noble altruist she had imagined, he has disclosed himself as an egoist, who only cares about appearances. Rejecting her relationship with Helmer, Nora leaves her husband and children in order to 'educate' herself.

As is evident from this outline, Krogstad is the major agent in the plot, while Rank's part in it is minute and only indirect. It is also apparent that Ibsen moves from a fairly superficial type of suspense to more penetrating and worrying questions.

But we may look at the play from an even more reductive point of view. Narrative, Todorov claims, in its most basic form is a causal transformation of a situation through five stages:

1   a state of equilibrium at the outset;

2   a disruption of the equilibrium by some action;

3   a recognition that there has been a disruption;

4   an attempt to repair the disruption;

5   a reinstatement of the initial equilibrium.[1]

What makes *A Doll's House* so innovative – and so disturbing – is that the harmonising last stage is lacking. Far from reinstating an equilibrium, the play ends on a note of climactic disruption.

In any drama text we may distinguish between the 'primary text' and the 'secondary text'. By primary text is meant everything that is verbalised in a performance, that is, the dialogue; by secondary text that which is verbalised only in the drama text: stage- and acting-directions, play title, divisional markers (act, scene), cue designations, etc.[2] While parts of the secondary text – notably stage- and acting-directions – are transposed into audiovisual signs in performance, other parts – the list of *dramatis personae*, for example – are not communicated to the spectator unless (s)he has access to a theatre program.

Compared to earlier playwrights, Ibsen is generous in his use of stage- and acting-directions. This may be so either because he had a double audience in mind and wished to help the reader to visualise the plays. Or it may reflect the fact that lacking a stage director in the modern sense of the word, he felt the need to provide the actors with the most essential directions.[3] However, unlike the epic stage- and acting-directions of Bernard Shaw and Eugene O'Neill, almost all of Ibsen's directions are functional, that is, they can be transposed into audiovisual stage signs. Even if they are not followed in productions of the play, directors and scenographers need to clarify to themselves what the playwright has intended with these directions, for you cannot 'understand what the characters *say* … unless you can read the visual *context* in which it is said'.[4] This must not be understood as a plea for slavish adherence to Ibsen's stage-directions;

it merely means that an awareness of the interplay that exists in the drama text between the characters and the setting is essential for a deeper understanding of the play. A thorough awareness of this interaction should therefore precede any production of it.

In his 'Notes for the Tragedy of Modern Times' Ibsen had written: 'There are two kinds of spiritual laws, two kinds of conscience, one for men and one, quite different, for women.' Since this difference is, partly at least, socially determined, it is significant that already in the hierarchically composed list of *dramatis personae*, the men are formally separated from the women; literally translated the list reads:

> Lawyer [*advokat*] Helmer
> Nora, his wife
> Doctor Rank
> Mrs Linde
> Lawyer [*sagfører*] Krogstad
> The Helmers' three small children
> Anne-Marie, nurse at the Helmers'
> The Maid, at the same place
> A Porter

All the men except the anonymous Porter are here introduced by profession plus surname. And it should be noticed that professional indications are in Norwegian used as a form of address: 'Would Lawyer Helmer be so kind as to …' Or even: 'Would the Lawyer be so kind as to …' The social status of the men is in this way more clearly advertised in the Norwegian original than in the English translations.

There is also an interesting parallel-by-contrast between Helmer's and Krogstad's professions, not visible in the English translations. Both are lawyers, but whereas Helmer as a barrister is qualified to plead before the Supreme Court, Krogstad lacks this qualification. As in the case of their banking experience and ambitions – Krogstad has hopes of being able to run the Credit Bank instead of Helmer –

Ibsen provides them with more or less identical professions, while at the same time indicating Helmer's social superiority.

One of the women, Mrs Linde, may formally seem to fall into the same category as the men, but her title indicates simply that she is – or, as the case is, has been – married. It thus denotes the same dependence on the male gender as the indication that Nora is Helmer's wife.

Of the three remaining women, two – Nora and Anne-Marie – are mentioned only by Christian name, while the third, the Maid, is nameless. (In the dialogue, she is addressed as 'Helene'.) To emphasise Nora's doll aspect, Ibsen uses the shortened pet form of the name rather than the full one, Eleonora. It is interesting to see that her adopted surname, Helmer, derived from Old Norse *helmr*, meaning 'helmet', is actually a male Christian name. The male dominance within the marriage is, in other words, strongly indicated already in Nora's two names – while her husband's authoritarian masculinity is advertised not only in his surname but also in his Christian name, Torvald, a compound derived from two Old Norse words: *þórr*, the god of thunder, and *vald* 'power'. 'Krogstad' indicates that its bearer is *kroget*, a Danish word meaning both literally and figuratively 'crooked' (cf. Norwegian *krokstav*, 'crook'). By contrast, 'Rank' means 'erect', a rather ironical name for a man suffering from inherited syphilis but figuratively speaking adequate. As we shall see, the name symbolism is meaningful not only when related to the men but also when related to Nora who is at once 'crooked' and – basically – 'erect'. Or, to put it differently, who changes from crookedness to erectness. Turning to the cue designations, we find a similar pattern: 'Helmer', 'Rank', 'Krogstad' as opposed to 'Mrs Linde', 'Nora', 'Nurse' and 'Maid'. Significantly, Nora is alone here in carrying a Christian name. No doubt the difference in cue designations between her and her husband serves to indicate not only the hierarchy within the marriage – Nora playing the role of 'daughter' to Helmer – but also the contrast between her (female) individualism and Helmer's socially determined (male) role of *paterfamilias*.

The appellation 'Nora' may also be seen as an anticipation of her final individualist 'revolt', since at the end of the play she is single: Nora.

When discussing the characters of *A Doll's House*, critics on the whole stick to the cue designations opted for by the playwright. The notable exception is Helmer, who is often – especially in more recent studies – referred to by his Christian name: Torvald. This usage reflects the modern view that the husband is not so much a pillar of society as a victim of it. However, deeming it wise to be consistent with Ibsen's own practice, I shall in the following consequently use the surname for the husband, the first name for the wife.

How old are the characters in *A Doll's House*? Ibsen never tells us explicitly but by combining scraps of information in the text we can draw certain conclusions. Given the fact that Nora has been married to Helmer for eight years, she can hardly be younger than twenty-four and she could be around thirty. The fact that she is an old friend of Mrs Linde, who cannot be very young, suggests rather that they are of about the same age.[5]

We may take for granted that Helmer is older than Nora, especially when we consider his promotion to bank manager. The fact that Rank has been his 'best friend from childhood' and that Krogstad has been a friend of his in his youth suggest that the three are of about the same age.

There is, in fact, much to be said for the idea that Helmer, Rank, Krogstad and Mrs Linde are all of about the same age, let us say around forty. Since the Nurse, Anne-Marie, must be even older, Nora finds herself surrounded by people who are considerably older than herself, a circumstance that presumably increases her feeling that she is being treated like a doll.

But age may also connote psychological relations. A Helmer of fifty rather than forty is a more obvious father substitute for a Nora of twenty-four rather than thirty. And a Rank of fifty may, in his way, fulfil a similar psychological role.

On the other hand, Helmer's paternalistic way of treating his wife

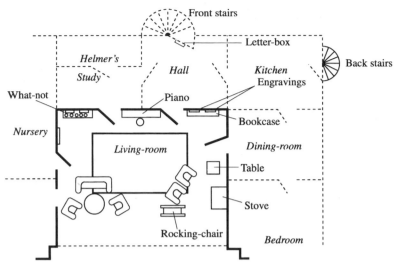

Floor plan for *A Doll's House*

would seem more disagreeable when there is no great age difference between them. If we regard *A Doll's House* primarily as a play about the suppressed position of woman in a male society, such a symbolic levelling of ages would help to accentuate the message.

Ibsen's description of the setting is, as usual, fairly detailed:

> *(A pleasantly and tastefully, but not expensively furnished living-room. A door to the right in the background leads to the hall; another door to the left in the background leads to* HELMER'*s study. Between these two doors a piano. In the middle of the left wall a door, with a window downstage of it. Near the window, a round table with armchairs and a small sofa. In the right wall, slightly upstage, is a door; downstage of this, against the same wall, a stove lined with porcelain tiles, with a couple of armchairs and a rocking-chair in front of it. Between the stove and the side door a small table. Engravings on the walls. A what-not with china and other bric-à-brac; a small bookcase with books in handsome bindings. Carpet on the floor; a fire in the stove. A winter's day.)*

On the basis of these stage-directions, where left and right mean 'as seen by the audience',[6] as well as from the implicit stage-directions found in the primary text, a floor plan may be designed (see figure p. 18). The very first sentence of the stage-directions reveals the author–narrator's point of view. The playwright makes the *reader* visualise a pleasant and tasteful room. At the same time he suggests to the director and the scene-designer that they recreate a pleasant and tasteful room on the stage for the *spectator*. While the reader can easily accept the idea, since the narrator's description allows him or her to imagine what *(s)he* finds pleasant and tasteful, the spectator who is confronted with a visual concretisation of the room may experience it as unpleasant and tasteless. Judging by the way people furnish their living-rooms, taste varies considerably.

When first confronted with this living-room, we find it hard to see much significance in it. It is said to be attractive – as a room in a doll's house is likely to be. The piano (music), the engravings (art) and the books (literature) suggest that at least one of the inhabitants has cultural interests. That is about all. Again there is a discrepancy between the reader and the spectator. The latter will neither be immediately aware of what is behind the doors in the background nor of the fact that it is '*a winter's day*'.

However, when we reread the play, the setting takes on a greater significance. We can now see that the room is an expression of Helmer's rather than Nora's taste. *He* is the ruler in this household and *he* is the one who explicitly voices his aesthetic interests. Therefore, as Helmer is gradually revealed as a man hiding behind a socially impeccable façade, the living-room takes on other qualities. The properties we took to be signs of genuine cultural interests now appear to be merely status objects, social icons. Like the play title, the setting is thus vested by Ibsen with a concealed pejorative meaning.

We may also ascribe the fact that the whole action takes place in one and the same room as a sign that Nora is imprisoned in a doll's house existence – although the room has 'no fewer than four doors, one of which leads to a fifth and a sixth'.[7] This raises the question of whether this is an open or a closed environment.

In order to get a clear picture of the structure, we need to divide the play into sequences. By 'sequence' is meant a section whose beginning and end, from the recipient's point of view, are determined by at least one of the following circumstances: (a) one or more entrances/exits (change of character constellation), (b) change of place, (c) change of time, marked by curtain or blackout.[8]

A Doll's House comprises seventy-seven sequences, as shown in the sequence scheme, pp. 169–72. As appears from this scheme, the length of the sequences varies a great deal, from one or two lines to ten pages. Most of the sequences are very brief and are inserted to satisfy the demands for realistic plausibility. An obvious example of such 'transitory sequences' are the fourteen appearances of the Maid, who usually enters merely to announce and let in visitors. Next to the great number of transitory sequences there is a small number of 'key sequences'. Between these two extremes we find a number of sequences which are of importance primarily for the forwarding of the plot, let us call them 'plot sequences'. Although there are no clear-cut border lines between the three kinds, the categorisation is useful since it helps us to see how Ibsen has built his play.

The sequence scheme gives a clear picture of the characters' stage presence. Nora appears in no less than seventy sequences, Helmer in thirty, Mrs Linde in twenty-one, the Maid in fourteen, Rank in twelve, Krogstad in six, the Helmers' children in five, the Nurse in four, the Porter in two. This should be compared to the number of speeches given to each character. The Porter has merely one speech, the Children three, the Nurse fifteen, the Maid sixteen. Although this quantitative distribution gives an idea of the relative importance of each character, it must be correlated with the number of lines given to each character and to the content of the speeches. Taking these factors also into account, we discover that while the Maid has a purely dramaturgic function, ushering visitors in and out, the Nurse has a thematic one and is consequently of greater interest.

Basic for the play structure is the ordering of the twelve key sequences (indicated by asterisks in the sequence scheme):

Act	Seq.	On stage				Length	Topic
I	8	N	H			4 p.	N's and H's present
	11	N		ML		10 p.	N's and H's past
	21	N			K	6 p.	K dismissed, N's forgery
	27	N	H			3 p.	K's forgery
II	34	N		ML		4 p.	N's loan
	39	N				R	4p.	R's illness and love for N
	46	N			K	3 p.	N's forgery
	52	N	H			R	2 p.	N's tarantella
III	60			ML K		4 p.	ML's and K's past, their reunion
	67	N	H			R	2 p.	R's final visit
	70	N	H			2 p.	K's two letters
	74	N	H			8 p.	N's and H's past

Interspersed between these key sequences are the transitory and plot sequences. Not surprisingly Nora appears in eleven of the twelve key sequences, securing a unity-of-character in the play. This directs our attention to sequence 60, where she does not appear. What is the justification for this sequence? Obviously, to provide an ironical contrast to Nora's and Helmer's separation. The relationship between Mrs Linde and Krogstad actually constitutes a subplot in the play.

Of special interest are the solo sequences. There are no less than sixteen such sequences, thirteen for Nora, two for Helmer and one for Mrs Linde. Solo sequences are permissible in illusionistic drama, provided they can be realistically accounted for. They may be silent (pantomimic) or they may be accompanied by speech (soliloquial). Even soliloquies may be justified in illusionistic drama – as Strindberg demonstrates in his famous preface to *Miss Julie* (1888) – when it can be made credible that a character would speak aloud to himself, as when drunk or insane.

But the characters in *A Doll's House* are neither drunk nor insane when they voice their soliloquies. This is how Act III opens:

MRS LINDE (*looks at her watch*) Not yet. There's not much time left. I
   hope he hasn't – (*Listens again.*) Ah, there he is. (*seq.59*)

From a strict naturalistic point of view, this soliloquy is hardly satisfactory. Mrs Linde is here voicing what in ordinary life would be silent thoughts. Much the same is true of Helmer's concluding soliloquy:

HELMER (*sinks down on a chair by the door and buries his face in his hands*)
   Nora! Nora! (*Looks around and gets up.*) Empty. She's not here anymore.
   (*With a glimmer of a hope.*) The most wonderful thing – ?! (*seq.77*)

However, in both cases one might argue that the characters are in a high state of tension, which results in a verbalisation of their thoughts.

Inner tension bordering on hysteria is certainly the realistic justification for Nora's thirteen soliloquies. The distribution is interesting. The first brief soliloquy comes exceedingly close to the conventional thought aside:

(*She continues to laugh happily to herself as she removes her coat,
etc. She takes from her pocket a bag containing macaroons and eats a
couple. Then she tiptoes across and listens at her husband's door.*) Yes,
he's at home. (*Starts humming again as she goes over to the
table, right.*) (*seq.6*)

Embedded in realistic stage business, the brief line serves to inform us that Helmer is at home – and that macaroons therefore cannot be eaten freely. The purpose of the line is purely expository; it is not psychologically justified.

The second soliloquy reveals Nora's reaction to Krogstad's threat:

NORA (*stands for a moment in thought, then tosses her head*) What nonsense! He's trying to frighten me! I'm not that stupid. (*Busies herself gathering together the children's clothes; then she suddenly stops.*) But – ? No, it's impossible. I did it for love, didn't I? (*seq.22*)

Nora's stage business indicates that the children are on her mind as she is trying to repress her anguish; it prepares for her verbalised worry for them in sequence 31.

The next one-word soliloquy demonstrates Nora's protest against her own anguish:

(*She sits on the sofa, takes up her embroidery, stitches for a few moments, but soon stops.*)
NORA No! (*Throws the embroidery aside, gets up, goes to the door leading to the hall and calls.*) Helen! Bring in the Christmas tree! (*seq.24*)

The Christmas tree must no longer be kept hidden. Nora will not let Krogstad interfere with family happiness. This decision is developed in the following soliloquy:

NORA (*busy decorating the tree*) Now – candles here – and flowers here. That loathsome man! Nonsense, nonsense, there's nothing to be frightened about. The Christmas tree must be beautiful. I'll do everything that you like, Torvald. I'll sing for you, dance for you – (*seq.26*)

A beautiful adorned Christmas tree, singing and dancing – Nora is emphatically defending her doll's life against the intruder. But Helmer, unwittingly, breaks down her defence when he condemningly describes Krogstad's crime in terms that fit Nora's. His remark that 'nearly all young criminals are the children of mothers who are constitutional liars' affects Nora's next two soliloquies:

NORA (*softly, after a pause*) It's nonsense. It must be. It's impossible. It *must* be impossible! (*seq.28*)

NORA (*pale with fear*) Corrupt my little children – ! Poison my home! (*Short pause. She throws back her head.*) It isn't true! It *couldn't* be true!

(*seq.30*)

Although Krogstad and Helmer oppose one another, they both appear as Nora's antagonists from now on. Male rationality is pitted against female intuition.

Act II opens with a soliloquy showing Nora's fear that Krogstad will drop a letter in the letter-box, whereby her forgery will be revealed to Helmer:

> (*She is alone in the room, walking restlessly to and fro. At length she stops by the sofa and picks up her coat.*)
> NORA (*drops the coat again*) There's someone coming! (*Goes to the door and listens.*) No, it's no one. Of course – no one'll come today, Christmas Day. Nor tomorrow. But perhaps – ! (*Opens the door and looks out.*) No. Nothing in the letter-box. Quite empty. (*Walks across the room.*) Silly, silly. Of course he won't do anything. It couldn't happen. It isn't possible. Why, I've three small children.   (*seq.31*)

As her handling of the coat clarifies, Nora does not dare to leave the apartment for fear that Krogstad will arrive while she is out. She is now literally imprisoned in her own home. What is already on her mind in this sequence becomes explicit in the next soliloquy:

> NORA (*begins to unpack the clothes from the box, but soon throws them down again*) Oh, if only I dared go out! If I could be sure no one would come and nothing would happen while I was away! Stupid, stupid! No one will come. I just mustn't think about it. Brush this muff. Pretty gloves, pretty gloves! Don't think about it, don't think about it! One, two, three, four, five, six – (*Cries.*) Ah – there they are – !   (*seq.33*)

The counting seems here merely an expression of Nora's attempt to rid herself of disturbing thoughts. Or is she counting the hours of her remaining life (cf. seq. 57), already here contemplating suicide? Her outburst is obviously caused by a sound she has heard from the hall. But who are 'they'? Nora may be thinking of Helmer and Rank who both enter from the hall a little later. But in view of her hysterical reaction, she may well be fearing that Krogstad has reported her crime to the police and that they are now coming to fetch her.[9]

The next soliloquy reveals that Nora interprets Helmer's assurance that he is 'man enough to bear the burden for us both' as a sign that he will sacrifice himself for her when it becomes known that Nora has committed forgery:

NORA (*desperate with anxiety, stands as though transfixed, and whispers*)
    He said he'd do it. He will do it. He will do it, and nothing'll stop him.
    No, never that. I'd rather anything. There must be some escape – Some
    way out – !
    (*The bell rings in the hall.*)
NORA   Dr Rank – ! Anything but that! Anything, I don't care – ! (*She
    passes her hand across her face, composes herself, walks across and opens
    the door to the hall.*)   (*seq.38*)

Nora's illusions about Helmer's noble nature are followed by a statement revealing her own noble mind. She decides not to make use of Rank's tender feelings for her by asking him for a loan to cover her debt to Krogstad. Note how Ibsen has Nora mention Rank's name even before he enters. Her claim that she has recognised his ringing should not be taken at its face value. It is Nora's way of denying to Rank and to herself that he is on her mind, as a potential money-lender.

Nora's anguish at the message that Krogstad has returned by 'the back way' is verbalised in the following soliloquy:

NORA   It's happening. It's happening after all. No, no, no, it can't
    happen, it mustn't happen. (*She walks across and bolts the door of
    HELMER's study.*)   (*seq.44*)

Nora then reveals, first her worry that Krogstad will drop the fatal letter in the letter-box, then her anguish when it becomes clear that he has indeed done so:

NORA (*runs to the hall door, opens it a few inches and listens*) He's going.
    He's not going to give him the letter. Oh, no, no, it couldn't possibly
    happen. (*Opens the door, a little wider.*) What's he doing? Standing

outside the front door. He's not going downstairs. Is he changing his
mind? Yes, he – !
(*A letter falls into the letter-box.* KROGSTAD's *footsteps die away down
the stairs.*)
NORA (*with a stifled cry, runs across the room towards the table by the
sofa. A pause*) In the letter-box. (*Steals timidly over towards the hall
door.*) There it is! Oh, Torvald, Torvald! Now we're lost!   (*seq.47*)

The last sentence prepares for the soliloquy with which Nora
provides a strong curtain for Act II. Here she shows herself calmly
desperate:

NORA (*stands for a moment as though collecting herself. Then she looks at her
watch*) Five o'clock. Seven hours till midnight. Then another twenty-
four hours till midnight tomorrow. And then the tarantella will be
finished. Twenty-four and seven? Thirty-one hours to live.   (*seq.57*)

As this soliloquy clarifies, she has decided to prevent Helmer from
sacrificing himself for her by sacrificing herself for him. Suicide is on
her mind. By linking the tarantella to her last hour of life, Ibsen
indicates its symbolic nature. It is a dance of death.

Nora's final soliloquy occurs midway through Act III:

NORA (*wild-eyed, fumbles around, seizes* HELMER's [*black*] *cloak, throws it
round herself and whispers quickly, hoarsely*) Never see him again. Never.
Never. Never. (*Throws the* [*black*] *shawl over her head.*) Never
see the children again. Them, too. Never. Never. Oh – the icy black
water! Oh – that bottomless – that – ! Oh, if only it were all over! Now
he's got it – he's reading it. Oh no, no! Not yet! Goodbye Torvald!
Goodbye my darlings! (*She turns to run into the hall.*)   (*seq.69*)

Her suicidal thoughts at this point are motivated by three ideas: she
must herself take full responsibility for what she has done; a suicide
on her part will demonstrate her love for Helmer and prevent him
from sacrificing himself for her; being a dangerous influence to her
own children, she can better disappear. Since Rank has just revealed
that he is soon to die, two more reasons for Nora's suicide may be

discerned: the loss of her best friend makes life less desirable for her; and Rank's stoic acceptance of a death caused by his father's licentiousness sets an example for Nora, who may see herself as a similar victim of paternal irresponsibility. The last reason especially indicates that Rank has, after all, a certain role in the plot of the play, albeit a momentary one since Nora later refrains from the idea of suicide.

Nora's final soliloquy, in which she still clings to her illusions about Helmer's noble mind, coincides with his offstage reading of Krogstad's first letter. His reaction to this letter, combined with his reaction to Krogstad's second one, opens her eyes to his true nature. She can now face her husband directly. Soliloquy is replaced by dialogue.

Nora's soliloquies 'tell us vaguely the source and intensity of her torment'.[10] The basic reason for their inclusion is the need to keep the recipient gradually informed about her increasingly anguished reactions to the threats launched at her. In that sense they are part of the plot.

Consider Ibsen's problem. He had chosen a protagonist who lives the life of a doll but has the makings of a mature human being. In her relations to other people Nora shows merely a veneer, a façade. Suddenly, at the end of the play, she reveals her true self. As a conventional dramaturgic device, a stage soliloquy serves primarily to reveal the true nature of the soliloquiser. By showing us glimpses of Nora's true self, a self hidden to the other characters, Ibsen could prepare for the climactic settlement sequence (seq. 74) where Nora finally reveals her real nature.

How plausible are the soliloquies from a realistic point of view? Their illusionistic justification is that Nora is childish and in pain.[11] However, it is doubtful whether the soliloquies, even with this argument, are realistically satisfying. Too long and too orderly to be altogether plausible, Nora's soliloquies are in fact included primarily to indicate her inner development and thus to prepare for her final transformation. This need for psychological motivation was so great that Ibsen had to sacrifice more superficial goals, such as realistic plausibility.

The central theme of the play hinges on the 'two kinds of conscience' Ibsen speaks of in his preliminary notes: Nora's individualist ethics versus Helmer's socially determined ones. The conflict, as old as drama itself, can be traced all the way back to Sophocles' *Antigone*. To Helmer Nora's forgery is a criminal act that cannot be excused; to Nora it is an act fully justified by the circumstances. Aware that she has done it to save her husband's life, Nora is even proud of her action. For once she has been able to do something for her husband – without his knowing it. The forgery is both an act of love and an act of independence, and it is difficult to say what is most important to Nora.

From the very beginning the situation is highly ironical. Reflecting the views of a male society, everyone sees Nora as a child to be cared for like a doll. Limited to a family environment, she has few possibilities to satisfy her need for self-respect. Even her children are taken care of by others. No wonder she relishes her secret knowledge that she has performed an independent act of extreme altruism, an act that is her pride not least because it creates a balance within the marriage. Seemingly totally dependent on her husband, Nora knows that at least once in his life Helmer has been totally dependent on her.

In Nora's little world there are few people she can feel attached to. Outside this world are the 'strangers'. Already in the beginning of the play Nora reveals her concern for those who are close to her and her indifference to those who are not:

HELMER ... Suppose I were to borrow a thousand crowns today, and you spent it all over Christmas, and then on New Year's Eve a tile fell off a roof on to my head –

NORA (*puts her hand over his mouth*) Oh, Torvald! Don't say such dreadful things!

HELMER Yes, but suppose something like that did happen? What then?

NORA   If anything as frightful as that happened, it wouldn't make much difference whether I was in debt or not.

HELMER   But what about the people I'd borrowed from?

NORA   Them? Who cares about them? They're strangers [*fremmede*].

HELMER   Oh, Nora, Nora, how like a woman!   (*seq. 8*)

Here the small 'female' world, where emotions are essential, is contrasted with the larger 'male' one, where rational thinking is of fundamental importance. You could also say that Nora represents a natural view (in the Darwinian sense), Helmer a social one.

Nora's indifference to strangers shows again when she suggests to Helmer that he 'get rid of one of the other clerks instead of Krogstad' (seq. 35). Similarly, in her controversy with Krogstad we are reminded that she has been indifferent to his children:

NORA   Show some heart, then. Think of my little children.

KROGSTAD   Have you and your husband thought of mine?   (*seq.46*)

Echoing their mother, Nora's children speak of 'the strange gentleman' (*den fremmede mand*) when they refer to Krogstad (seq. 23). And even Helmer wishes to avoid 'outside influences' (*fremmede indflydelser*).

The theme reaches its climax at the end of the play when Nora declares that 'for eight years' she has been living 'with a complete stranger', that she 'can't spend the night in a strange man's house', and that she does not accept anything from 'strangers'. Not least in view of her earlier use of the word, Nora's emotional distance from her husband at this point is clear. Ibsen here reverses the situation of Euripides' *Alcestis*, in which the husband discovers in the Stranger his lost wife. In Ibsen's 'new recognition scene the wife discovers the Stranger in her own husband'.[12]

Fundamental to the play structure is Ibsen's construction of situations for the characters surrounding Nora which in one way or another illustrate her predicament.[13] Thus Nora and Mrs Linde are parallel figures moving in opposite directions. When the play begins, Mrs Linde turns to Nora for help. Both midway through the play and at the end of it, it is Nora's turn to ask Mrs Linde for help. Mrs Linde gains a family; Nora loses one.

If one does not perceive this parallel, the initial conversation between Nora and Mrs Linde seems needlessly circumstantial. When Mrs Linde first appears, in the evening, she '*is dressed in travelling clothes*'. When Nora leaves her house at night she is dressed in '*outdoor clothes*' and carries '*a small travelling-bag*'. Mrs Linde's arrival at the Helmers' is described as follows:

MRS LINDE (*shyly and a little hesitantly*) Good evening, Nora.

NORA (*uncertainly*) Good evening –

MRS LINDE I don't suppose you recognise me.

NORA No, I'm afraid I – Yes, wait a minute – surely – ! (*Exclaims.*) Why, Christine! Is it really you?

MRS LINDE Yes, it's me.

NORA Christine! And I didn't recognise you ! But how could I – ? (*More quietly.*) How you've changed, Christine!

MRS LINDE Yes, I know. (*seq. 11*)

The reason Nora does not recognise Mrs Linde immediately is, of course, that the two have not seen one another for many years. But this realistic explanation is not sufficient. The essential reason is that it enables us to see, retroactively, that Mrs Linde at this point appears to Nora as unrecognisable as Nora does to Helmer at the end of the play. Nora's reference to Mrs Linde's drastic change exactly corresponds to Helmer's feelings about Nora at the end – as well as to her feelings about him. In short, Nora's reaction to Mrs Linde highlights the theme of estrangement. By indicating Mrs Linde's outward change – which mirrors an inner one – it also points to the mental change both Nora and Helmer must undergo to create a true relationship. This parallel helps to integrate Mrs Linde in the play. In addition it creates an ironical, even mystical feeling that life repeats itself and that our fates as human beings are exchangeable.

Ibsen then continues to develop the parallel:

NORA (*quietly*) Poor Christine, you've become a widow. … Oh, my
poor darling, what you've gone through! And he didn't leave you
anything?

MRS LINDE No.

NORA No children, either?

MRS LINDE No.

NORA Nothing at all, then?

MRS LINDE Not even a feeling of loss or sorrow.

NORA (*looks incredulously at her*) But, Christine, how is that
possible?

MRS LINDE (*smiles sadly and strokes* NORA's *hair*) Oh, these things
happen, Nora.

NORA All alone. How dreadful that must be for you. I've three
lovely children. (*seq. 11*)

Like Mrs Linde in the beginning, Nora at the end, leaving her husband and her three children, is 'all alone'. The '*large black shawl*' she
then '*puts on*' and the '*small travelling-bag*' she carries in her hand
visually turn her into a disinherited 'widow'. But unlike Mrs Linde,
she is deliberately disinherited. It is as though Mrs Linde, who after
all is the one who decides that Nora should tell her husband the
truth, has infused Nora with the will-power she herself has lacked
with regard to *her* husband. Knowing what it means to remain in an
unhappy marriage – she here anticipates Mrs Alving in *Ghosts* – Mrs
Linde is anxious to help Nora out of one.

Like the initial conversation between Nora and Mrs Linde, that
between Nora and the nurse Anne-Marie (seq. 32) illuminates the
ending. 'How could you bear to give your child away – to strangers?'
Nora asks the Nurse. She is already contemplating leaving her own
children. When she does it, at the end, she repeatedly insists, as we
have seen, that her husband has become 'a stranger' to her. Since the
children will henceforth be brought up by Helmer and the Nurse,
Nora in a sense gives her children away to 'strangers'. Another parallel consists in the fact that just as Nora herself was brought up by her
father and the Nurse, who was her substitute mother, so her children

will be brought up by the same kind of 'parents'. There is presumably considerable consolation to Nora in the fact that the Nurse who has cared so lovingly for her as a child will now care for her children. If this had not been the situation, Nora might not have found it possible to leave her family.

What Anne-Marie, Mrs Linde and Nora have in common is their altruism with regard to those who are close to them, Anne-Marie with regard to Nora as a child, Mrs Linde with regard to her mother and brothers, Nora with regard to her husband. Together they incarnate 'la condition féminine'.[14]

Both Helmer and Mrs Linde claim that Nora is a great spendthrift – as her father was. And Nora's all too generous tipping of the Porter may seem to confirm their statements. But Helmer does not know as yet that Nora has actually been saving most of the money he has given her to be able to pay off her debt to Krogstad. There is, in other words, only an apparent parallel between Nora and her father in this respect. The same goes for the crime the father has committed and which has been covered up by the 'righteous' Helmer. While Helmer naturally sees a parallel between the father's crime and Nora's – the sin of the father being inherited by his child – the recipient is more inclined to link the father's forgery with Krogstad's. The reason Ibsen slips in the information about the father's crime is not that it highlights Nora's crime but that it illuminates Helmer's double morals. For when Helmer later shows himself anxious to cover up Nora's crime, he is repeating his behaviour with regard to her father. When put to the test, he again reveals himself as morally weak, preferring appearances to truth.

More obvious than these parallels is the one between Nora and Krogstad. Both are socially dependent on Helmer, he by being his employee, she by being his wife. By making them both guilty of the same crime, and by confronting their 'boss' with both crimes, Ibsen reveals Helmer's ethical inconsistency to us.

Like Nora, Krogstad has secretly committed a forgery. When Helmer informs Nora about this, he strongly condemns not so much the act itself as the fact that Krogstad has kept it secret; it is this secrecy, Helmer claims, that 'has morally destroyed him'. For years, Helmer tells his wife, Krogstad has been 'poisoning his children with his lies and pretences'.

There are, dramaturgically speaking, at least two reasons why Helmer is arguing in this manner. First, Nora at this point must be put under pressure; unwittingly, Helmer is admonishing her to confess or even to leave her family which she has been 'poisoning' for years. Second, Helmer's reasoning at this point means that he can still be seen by Nora – and possibly by us – as morally high-minded. As a result, his hypocrisy becomes retrospectively all the more flagrant when, in Act III, he gladly accepts Krogstad's offer to keep Nora's crime hidden to the world.

Krogstad himself has earlier told Nora that his crime has socially destroyed him. His criticism of the stern norms of society is pitted against Helmer's condemning of Krogstad's individual morals. At the end of Act I, Nora is caught between these conflicting views.

It is, however, as I have already indicated, doubtful whether Krogstad's crime can be equated with Nora's. The relevant passage reads:

KROGSTAD Mrs Helmer, you evidently don't appreciate exactly what you have done. But I can assure you that it is no bigger nor worse a crime than the one I once committed and thereby ruined my whole social position.

NORA You? Do you expect me to believe that you would have taken a risk like that to save your wife's life?

KROGSTAD The law does not concern itself with motives.

NORA Then the law must be very stupid. *(seq.21)*

Krogstad's description of the law – which obviously does not agree with the real-life situation even in 1879 – serves to contrast a moral view that 'does not concern itself with motives' (Helmer's morals) with one that does (Nora's morals). Since Krogstad avoids answering Nora's question directly, we may assume that *his* forgery, unlike hers, was of an egoistic kind. (If Ibsen had wished to demonstrate a complete parallel between the two crimes, it would have been very easy for him to begin Krogstad's second speech above with 'I do, but the law …') This being the case, it would be quite legitimate for Helmer to judge Krogstad's crime much more harshly than he does Nora's identical one. But Helmer's distinction between them has nothing to do with the 'motives' of the criminals and everything to do with their position in relation to himself. Ironically, Nora's indictment of Krogstad – 'You must be a rotten lawyer' – is highly applicable to Helmer. Another irony is that Krogstad now treats Nora the way he himself has been treated. There is a note of revengeful equality-before-the-law in his harsh description of the legal system.

Nora and Rank, finally, are linked by the fact that they are both victims of their father's frivolity. Rank has inherited a mortal illness, syphilis, as a result of his father's licentiousness, an illness that was still incurable in the 1880s. As a result of her father's way of bringing her up – 'he played with me just the way I played with my dolls' – Nora has been introduced to a hierarchic system, where women are playthings and role-playing a matter of course. 'You and papa have done me a great wrong', she tells Helmer toward the end. 'It's your fault that I have done nothing with my life.' Be it biological heritage (Rank) or moral environment (Nora) – in either case it is the sins of the fathers, rather than those of the mothers as Helmer wants to have it, that have been visited upon their children.

Another important reason why Rank is included in the play is that he helps illuminate Nora's ethics, her way of dealing with someone who is not a stranger, someone who is close to her heart. After Rank has revealed to her that his days are numbered, she shows him her silk-stockings. Why? Is she 'prostituting' herself, playing on Rank's tender feelings for her, in the hope that this will make him more inclined to lend her the money she so badly needs? Or is she, on the contrary, now when she knows that he is soon going to die, offering him an implicit love declaration, so different from his explicit one? Rather than help her, his love declaration actually pre-

vents her from asking him to lend her the money. Why? Is it because
she is afraid of the scandal that might arise, will it be known that she
has received money from a secret admirer?[15] Is Nora another Hedda
Gabler? Or is it because she now intuitively refuses to trade money
for love, to make improper use of tender feelings she is not free to
return, thus revealing herself as 'one of those pure of heart'?[16] If the
latter interpretation seems more meaningful, it is because it suggests
that Nora's ability to resist Rank's offer forms a striking contrast to
Helmer's inability, in Act III, to resist Krogstad's threat. When it
comes to a real test, Nora's 'female' ethics prove to be substantial and
genuine – as Helmer's 'male' ones do not.

In order to see how carefully Ibsen has constructed his drama, we
need to look more closely at some of its parts.

The play opens on a harmonious note:

> (*A bell rings out in the hall; after a moment we hear a door being opened.*
> NORA *enters the living-room, humming contentedly to herself; she is*
> *wearing outdoor clothes and carrying a lot of parcels, which she puts*
> *down on the table right. She leaves the door to the hall open behind*
> *her and out there we can see a* PORTER *carrying a Christmas tree and a*
> *basket. He gives these to the* MAID, *who has opened up for them.*)
> NORA Hide the Christmas tree well, Helene. The children mustn't see it
> until tonight, when it's decorated. (*To the* PORTER, *taking out her purse.*)
> How much – ?
> PORTER Fifty øre.
> NORA Here's a crown. No, keep it all.
> (*The* PORTER *thanks and leaves.* NORA *closes the door.*)   (*seq. 1–5*)

This opening immediately suggests that it is Christmas Eve. It also
tells us that Nora tips the Porter more than one would normally do,
but we cannot make out why this is so. Is Nora a spendthrift? Is she
unusually generous because it is Christmas? (A third possibility –
that Nora is open-handed because her husband's financial position
has recently improved – is still unknown to us at this point.) But the
opening means more than this. This is the first monetary allusion in

the play and 'the references to money all lead into the play ... and culminate in Nora's "Torvald, this is a settling of accounts."'[17]

Important, too, is that already here one of the central symbols, the Christmas tree, is literally brought into the play, thereby receiving the needed attention from the recipient. The Christmas tree may be seen as a 'symbol of family happiness and security',[18] 'a natural product of the forests', which 'has been prevented from full growth, cut or transplanted, then prettified and decorated in a domestic environment, like Nora herself'.[19]

Indeed, as an exponent of the mask-versus-face theme of the play the tree especially relates to Nora:

> The Christmas tree ... is dressed and then stripped – which links it with the later fancy-dress ball and the costume Nora first dons and later discards. ... The 'real' tree for the children is to be the dressed tree, not its unadorned version. And this links the notion of dress and costume to that of deception and masquerade, which in turn links with Nora's deception of Torvald about borrowing money and Dr Rank's disguising for twenty [*sic*] long years his true feelings for Nora. This, in turn, makes us aware that some kinds of deception, like hiding the unadorned Christmas tree, can be for potentially good purposes.[20]

Eventually Nora's children enter the stage. Although the five sequences in which they appear (seq. 17–20, 23) are all quite brief, they are not insignificant, since they establish 'Nora's love for her children, so that when she walks out at the end, the audience has a vivid sense of what she is giving up'.[21] In addition, they demonstrate Nora's own childish nature, perhaps also her repressed aggressions: 'Have you been throwing snowballs? Oh, I wish I'd been there!' The central passage reads:

> The NURSE *brings the children into the room.* NORA *follows, and closes the door to the hall.*
>
> NORA How well you look! What red cheeks you've got! Like apples and roses!

The CHILDREN *in the following keep talking to her as she talks to them.*
NORA Have you had fun? That's splendid. You gave Emmy and Bob a ride
on the sledge? What, both together? I say! What a clever boy you are,
Ivar! Oh, let me hold her for a moment Anne-Marie! My sweet little
doll-child! (*Takes the smallest child from the* NURSE *and dances with her.*
(*seq. 18*)

As Nora closes the door, the living-room is turned into a playroom.
The roles of mother and servant are strictly divided, the servant *cares*
for the children, the mother *plays* with them. The roles even seem
unnaturally reversed when the mother asks the servant for permission to hold her own child.

Nora's dancing with her 'doll-child' relates to Helmer's accompanying of his 'doll-wife' on the piano as she is dancing the tarantella.
The hide-and-seek Nora is soon to play with her children dramatises
the hide-and-seek husband and wife are playing with one another.
More generally, Nora's playing with her children is a vivid symbol of
the Helmer family interaction; as Nora clarifies in her final settlement with her husband:

> … our home has never been anything but a playroom. I've been your
> doll-wife, just as I used to be papa's doll-child. And the children have
> been my dolls. I used to think it was fun when you came in and
> played with me, just as they think it's fun when I go in and play
> games with them. That's all our marriage has been, Torvald. (*seq. 74*)

This brings us to the tarantella sequences (seq. 52–3). On the most
obvious level, Nora dances the tarantella to distract Helmer's attention from the fateful letter-box. Her wild dancing expresses her fear
that he will discover her crime. Helmer is unable to guide Nora but
Rank, who is himself doomed to die shortly, is more successful.
Rank and Nora, both in the shadow of death, understand one
another intuitively. Helmer understands nothing. The many references to failed attempts at guidance help to pinpoint the fact that
Nora, although she has herself asked Helmer for it, no longer fol-

lows his instruction. Still admiring him – or trying to do so – she is instinctively breaking away from him. In this sense the tarantella prepares for her discovery at the end that she and her husband have in fact never understood one another.

The reason why Nora practises of all dances a tarantella is not so much that this rapid, whirling south Italian dance reminds Helmer and herself of their happy days in and around Naples. The tarantella, as used by Ibsen, is a sophisticated motif which demands of the recipient a certain factual knowledge both of the dance and of the spider that has given the dance its name:

> The tarantula spider is reputedly poisonous, and anyone bitten by it is likely to contract the disease of tarantism. This is 'a hysterical malady, characterized by an extreme impulse to dance'. And the cure for this malady was held to be – dancing the tarantella. Thus, 'the dancing was sometimes held to be a symptom or consequence of the malady, sometimes practised as a sovereign cure for it'. The symptom of the disease and the cure for the disease are one and the same.[22]

The wildness with which Nora dances the tarantella is indeed similar to what we would expect from someone bitten by the tarantula. Squeezed between Krogstad's demands and Helmer's stern moralising, she has got the poison in her system. Suicide is on her mind. And at the same time a vague hope that a miracle might save her. The tarantella is a fitting, theatrically powerful expression of her schizophrenic situation.

Nothing in the play has been so much discussed as the conclusion. Ibsen was himself well aware of its significance: 'I might almost say that it is precisely on account of the final scene that the whole play was written.'[23] By 'the final scene' Ibsen undoubtedly meant what we have here termed sequence 74. Nora's demand at this point that she and her husband sit down and talk seriously 'for the first time' signifies a crucial change in the development of the play as well as in her moral and social attitude. But it does not provide an answer to the major question we ask ourselves in the final act: Will Nora leave her husband and children? Not until we see her in her outdoor dress, carrying her travelling-bag – in the middle of the night! – is an answer, albeit inconclusive, provided.

Within this larger unit, comprising roughly the last two pages in the Norwegian standard edition, we may distinguish the *very end*, the actual leave-taking and exit, comprising the last six speeches plus stage- and acting-directions. In the following, I shall focus on this part of the ending; how it was first conceived by Ibsen; and how he later gave it an alternative form.

The passage that concerns us is the following:

HELMER Nora, – can I never be anything but a stranger to you?
    NORA (*picks up her bag*) Oh, Torvald, then the most wonderful thing would have to happen. –
HELMER Name it, this most wonderful thing!
    NORA You and I would both have to change so much that – . Oh, Torvald, I don't believe in wonders any more.
HELMER But I'll believe in them. Tell me! Change so much that – ?
    NORA That our life together could become a marriage. Goodbye. (*She leaves through the hall.*)
HELMER (*sinks down on a chair by the door and covers his face with his hands*) Nora! Nora! (*Looks around and gets up.*) Empty. She is no longer here. (*With a glimmer of hope.*) The most wonderful thing – ?! (*The sound of a street door being slammed shut is heard from below.*)

(*seq.76–7*)

Compare this to the ending in the first complete draft:

HELMER Nora, can I never be anything but a stranger to you?
    NORA Oh, Thorvald, then the most wonderful thing would have to happen. –
HELMER Name it, this most wonderful thing!
    NORA You and I would both have to change so much that; – oh, Thorvald, I don't believe in wonders any more.

HELMER But I believe in them! Tell me! Change so much that –

NORA That our life together could become a marriage. Goodbye. (*She quickly picks up her bag, waves and leaves.*)

HELMER (*sinks down on a chair by the door*) Nora! Nora! – The most wonderful thing – ?

Although the two texts may seem very similar, there are some notable differences between them. In the draft, Nora's leave-taking is somewhat hesitant: she picks up the bag immediately before leaving, she waves to Helmer and – most conspicuously – there is no door slam. In the published version, by contrast, Nora picks up the bag at an earlier point; she no longer waves to Helmer; and her departure not only shows greater determination on her part; it is also more definite. Ibsen very specifically informs us that the door not only slams shut but actually locks behind her – as though no return is possible.

While the Nora of the draft may well come back sooner or later, there are thus various indications in the published version that she will not. Her slamming of the door 'seems to summarize in a single action Nora's rejection of her husband, her children, her home and her social position, along with the society that taught her to need such things'. [24] Nora's exit through the front door of the apartment also significantly contrasts with her entrance through it in the opening of the play, when we see her happily returning home with a Christmas tree. 'The unadorned Christmas tree, framed in the doorway at the beginning of the play' is linked 'with the figure of Nora, no longer in fancy dress, passing through the same doorway at the end of the play'. [25]

As for Helmer, we may note that, whereas in the draft he claims to believe in miracles, in the final version this is weakened to a desire to believe in them; as a result the (added) acting-direction concerning the hope he suddenly clings to seems to be born more out of his desperation than out of faith. Taken together the nuances inserted by Ibsen considerably strengthen the ending in the published version, making it harsher, more provocative.

The fact that the Helmers live on one of the upper floors of an apartment house becomes especially meaningful at the end:

> When Nora walks out, we … get a feeling that she is going through … an initiation ritual with numerous stages – doorway, hall, door, hall, stairs, and final door for her escape to the outside. This is an aspect of the play where Ibsen had free choice; he could have given the Helmers a house, or even an apartment on the ground floor, without changing the play's surface at all. … The elaborate separation between the inner and the outer world increases the gaps between them; we feel that Nora's 'doll house' is a refuge from the cold, hard world outside, a safe haven – or a prison.[26]

Is the ending complete in the Aristotelian sense that it 'naturally follows some other thing, either by necessity or as a rule, but has nothing following it'?[27] There has been much speculation about what happens to Nora and Helmer after she has left him. In this sense the end of *A Doll's House* does have something 'following it'. Commenting on a play by his countryman Andreas Munch, Ibsen already in 1857 declared: 'the play does not end when the curtain falls after the fifth act; the real end is found outside the frame; the poet has indicated the direction in which we have to go; it is now our task, each for himself, to imagine it.'[28] This description excellently fits at least two of Ibsen's own plays.[29] Long before Brecht, he created provocative open endings in *A Doll's House* and in *Ghosts*. Both playwrights invite the recipient to take a stand.

However, after he had heard that *A Doll's House* had been produced in Germany with a changed ending, falsely attributed to him, Ibsen provided his play with an alternative ending. The situation arose when the actress playing the part of Nora, Hedwig Niemann-Raabe, feeling that in such a situation *she* would never have left *her* children, refused to play the ending as written.

To prevent any further hampering with his text by others, Ibsen preferred to commit what he in a public letter termed 'a barbaric act of violence' to the piece himself, adding that it was very much against his wish that the alternative ending be used.[30] His alternative German ending reads as follows in English translation:

NORA ... Where we could make a real marriage out of our lives together. Goodbye. (*Begins to go.*)

HELMER Go then! (*Seizes her arm.*) But first you shall see your children for the last time!

NORA Let me go! I will not see them! I cannot!

HELMER (*draws her over to the door, left*) You shall see them. (*Opens the door and says softly.*) Look, there they are asleep, peaceful and carefree. Tomorrow, when they wake up and call for their mother, they will be – motherless.

NORA (*trembling*) Motherless ...!

HELMER As you once were.

NORA Motherless! (*Struggles with herself, lets her travelling-bag fall and says.*) Oh, this is a sin against myself, but I cannot leave them. (*Half sinks down by the door.*)

HELMER (*joyfully, but softly*) Nora!

The curtain falls[31]

Most directors and actresses were not impressed by Ibsen's sentimental alternative ending. It was used only a few times, and eventually even Mrs Niemann-Raabe accepted the original ending.

Where does Nora go, once she has slammed the street door shut? To some critics this is an irrelevant question. Once the final curtain has come down, they claim, we know nothing about the future fate of the characters. As we have seen, the playwright himself held a different opinion. Moreover, this is overlooking what is explicitly stated in the text, where Nora makes it quite plain that she plans to spend the night at Mrs Linde's place and that she then intends to return to her childhood environment to look for a job there – a clear indication of her determination to 'educate' herself.

Nora's fighting spirit at the end contrasts markedly with the thoughts of suicide she has voiced earlier in the play. Once Helmer has revealed that he is not what she has imagined him to be, the self-sacrifice becomes pointless. When Nora at the end puts on the black shawl and exits through the dark hall, the costume and lighting are no signs that suicide is on her mind. They merely stress the sadness of what is happening, that a home is broken up. They may also be seen as a hint that the future in store for her will be a hard one.

Before leaving her family, Nora makes it completely clear why she does so. In the most provocative speech of the whole play, she tells her husband:

> You were perfectly right. I'm not fitted to educate them [the children]. There's something else I must do first. I must educate myself. And you can't help me with that. It's something I must do by myself. That's why I'm leaving you. (*seq.74*)

While Helmer, speaking for society at large, claims that a married woman is 'first and foremost ... wife and mother', Nora finds that she is 'first and foremost a human being'. That is, while motherhood to Helmer is a self-evident biological, gender-related phenomenon, to Nora it is above all a psychological, social and moral one, demanding 'education'. Her reasoning can be phrased in terms of a generalising syllogism:

1   To be a fit mother, a wife must have an identity as a human being.
2   In a male society a wife is denied such an identity.
3   Conclusion: A wife in a male society cannot be a fit mother.

This being the situation, the only thing Nora can do is to try to find her own identity in opposition to or at least unassisted by the society in which she lives – a tremendous task.

Naturally, self-identity has a value in itself. But it is important to see – as many critics blaming her for egoism have not – that Nora does not leave her family to discover her true self merely for her own sake. She does it in the conviction that self-knowledge is a prerequisite for being a true wife and mother. If any explication of the play text on this point is needed, there is Ibsen's statement to Erik af Edholm that 'with the view of her marriage which Nora has acquired in the course of that night, it would be immoral of her to continue living with Helmer. That she cannot do, and so she leaves'.[32]

It is, of course, possible to doubt Nora's motives and to argue that she is actually deluding herself. Lurking behind all her noble, democratic statements, we might suspect, is a desire to free herself from all responsibility. For many years she has been egoistically concerned with her own family, caring little for other people. Now she rejects even the ones nearest and dearest to herself. For what? What does it really mean, that self-education, that search for self-identity except narcissistically caring only about oneself? However, it takes a considerable reading against the text to interpret the play in this manner. Clearly, a Nora who is psychologically disarmed in this way is no threat at all to a male society. Rather than suspect the honesty of Nora's motives, we may suspect the motives lurking behind interpretations of this kind.

Besides, it is noteworthy that Nora finds that she has to 'educate' herself. The expression indicates that she is now prepared to become a social human being, caring for people also outside her family circle, people she has so far regarded as 'strangers'.

Another way of disarming the play of its explosive power is to declare that 'Ibsen is not writing about a "typical" woman responding to social and psychological forces, but about an exceptional one making a free, self-transforming decision.'[33] Naturally, Nora has her individual characteristics. She is a character in the round. She is even exceptional in certain ways. Most women do not commit forgery to save their men's lives. But then most women do not have a rich father dying at the same time as the life of their husband has to be saved. We are, after all dealing with a structured play, not with amorphous reality. But this does not mean that Nora's discriminated situation and her way of reasoning are exceptional. On the contrary, they have proved highly representative to 'a hundred thousand women', to quote Nora – if not to their husbands. If they had not been understood in this way, the play would never have had such a tremendous impact on generations of readers and spectators.

It is of course true that we can have no certain knowledge of Nora's future – or of Helmer's. Will she be able to educate herself and cope with her new situation?[34] And will he be able to cope with his? These are the questions we pose when the door has been slammed and the final curtain has dropped. As we have seen, the play text gives certain general indications in a positive direction with regard to her: Nora's honesty, seriousness and determination imply that she *will* manage.

Nevertheless, many commentators have seen Nora, even at the end, as a doll, badly equipped to cope with life outside her doll's house. To them it seems obvious that Nora will eventually return home to Helmer and the children. However, they often disagree about the nature of Nora's return. Theoretically there are three possibilities: (a) Nora returns to her earlier doll's role, (b) Nora takes over the regime, and (c) Nora helps establish a new relationship with her husband, based on equality.

In his discussion of the play, Strindberg settles for the last of these alternatives. His reason for wanting Nora to stay at home is seemingly well-founded, in the light of the play context: 'Once she has discovered what a dolt her husband is, there is all the more reason for her to stay with the children.' Yet the point Ibsen makes at the end is that Nora has little faith not only in Helmer's but also in her own ability to educate their children and that the Nurse will actually make a better 'parent' than either of them. 'The servants know about everything to do with the house – much better than I do', Nora tells her husband shortly before leaving.

Like Strindberg, Weigand sees little sense in Nora's departure. Speculating about her future fate, he writes:

> ... personally I am convinced that after putting Torvald through
> a sufficiently protracted ordeal of suspense, Nora will yield to his
> entreaties and return home – on her own terms.... For a time the
> tables will be reversed: a meek and chastened husband will eat out of

the hand of his squirrel; and Nora, hoping to make up by a sudden spurt of zeal for twenty-eight [*sic*] years of lost time, will be trying desperately hard to grow up. I doubt, however, whether her volatile enthusiasm will even carry her beyond the stage of resolutions. The charm of novelty worn off, she will tire of the new game very rapidly and revert, imperceptibly, to her role of song-bird and charmer, as affording an unlimited range to the exercise of her inborn talents of coquetry and play-acting.[35]

In this male chauvinist statement, Weigand clearly sees Nora's future as a combination of our point (b) and (a), whereas the play text, assuming that 'the most wonderful thing' will happen, suggests point (c). Weigand's 'conviction' seems to be founded more on his own wishful thinking than on what can be supported by the text. Obliquely condemning Nora's decision to leave her home, he is in fact commenting, not on the drama text but on a possible production based on it. Rather than interpreting the text, he is 'directing' it.

We find another kind of bias with Marxist critics. Bien categorically declares that Nora at the end leaves 'the bourgeois society not to return to it'.[36] But Nora is much more radical than this suggests. A Rousseauan at heart, she has misgivings about society in general, not just its bourgeois variety. And far from leaving society, she challenges it at the end: 'I must try to satisfy myself which is right, society or I.'

So far we have focused on Nora. What about Helmer? According to one critic, he is, once Nora has left him,

a bewildered and confused man who is still completely imprisoned within the conditioned assumptions of his middle-class world. Torvald, we now see, is as much a victim as Nora, but he has not even begun to understand his predicament. The play closes with a question mark left in the audience's mind. Will Torvald ever learn to see and to understand in the way that his wife has, or will he continue to allow his responses and actions to be controlled by social conditioning?[37]

This view of an essentially unchanged Helmer may seem quite valid. Yet to another critic Helmer suddenly does change at the end – 'the light begins to break on Torvald' – just as Krogstad does at the beginning of Act III.[38] Both critics partly opt for suggestive statements, relevant for many stagings of the play, rather than for open questions, more in tune with the rather noncommittal drama text, such as: Is the Helmer of the ending still 'completely imprisoned' in his middle-class world? Or does he begin to understand his predicament?

What kind of play is *A Doll's House*? In view of Ibsen's own experience as a stage manager, we would expect it to have some connection with the Scribean *pièce bien faite*. Ibsen's play has indeed certain traits in common with the well-made play.[39] There is the late point of attack – Nora's reunion with Mrs Linde after many years, motivating the unravelling of the past; the blackmail plot creating dramatic suspense; the *quid pro quo's*: Mrs Linde wrongly guessing the identity of Nora's creditor; and Nora's flirting with Rank resulting in an unwelcome love declaration.

The problem with all these devices is that, characteristic as they are of the well-made play, they appear also in other dramatic genres. Besides, Ibsen transcends the well-made play in making the plot subservient both to the portrayal of the protagonist and to the serious ethical and social problems raised in the play. He also transcends it by supplementing the unravelling in the third act – a standard feature of the *pièce bien faite* – with what Shaw terms 'discussion'.

While few would regard *A Doll's House* as a comedy,[40] most critics would agree that the play, up to a point, is a problem drama, that is, a drama concerned with social issues to which solutions are, or can be, found. George Steiner, for example, claims that the play 'is founded on the belief … that woman can and must be raised to the dignity of man'.[41] Viewed in this way, *A Doll's House* is a play which argues for equality between the sexes and which implies that, once this has been achieved, there is no need for Nora to leave her home since it has then ceased to be – a doll's house.

But this is certainly taking a one-sided and limited view of the play. Even in a society where equality has been achieved, the ethical problems raised in *A Doll's House* will continue to exist. Besides, both the moral stature and the complexity of Nora point away from problem drama – where ideas rather than characters stand central – in the direction of tragedy.

The concept of tragedy is problematic, especially in modern drama, and much depends on which criteria we attach to the term. Nora may certainly fulfil Aristotle's demand that the protagonist be morally superior to the average person, yet tainted by a flaw. But does her modest social status make her fit to be a tragic protagonist? And is Aristotle's demand that the action of tragedy be 'complete' in agreement with the open ending of *A Doll's House*? In both respects the play seems more akin to non-Aristotelian drama. If it is true that 'the essence of tragedy is the inescapability of the issue',[42] then it is doubtful whether *A Doll's House* can be called a tragedy. For what is inescapable here except Rank's, a minor character's, imminent death? If inescapability of the issue is a valid criterion for tragedy, then *Ghosts* would certainly make a better case. Northam argues that Nora's fight against fatality, 'a fight in which she will sacrifice no basic principles however desperate her situation, makes her into a heroine'.[43] But the fact that Nora remains outwardly undefeated hardly agrees with our notion of a *tragic* heroine. Raymond Williams points out that in Ibsenite 'liberal tragedy' the hero challenges 'an opposing world, full of lies and compromises and dead positions, only to find, as he struggles against it, that as a man he belongs to this world, and has its destructive inheritance in himself'.[44] This description with its allusion to the idea of Original Sin may well be true of many of Ibsen's plays. But it does not wholly fit *A Doll's House*, where the protagonist's determination to confront society and educate herself carries an optimistic note. The Nora who leaves her doll's house existence for a lonely one outside it is either unaware of the fact that she has the 'destructive inheritance' of this world planted in herself or, more likely, disagrees with this idea.

While no generic label wholly seems to fit *A Doll's House*, several have some justification in relation to it. Its plot relates to the well-made play, its theme to problem drama, and its delineation of characters, especially of the protagonist, to tragedy. There are comic moments in the play, and we may even argue that it begins as comedy and ends as close-to-tragedy. As we have seen, the ending is ambiguous in its openness. Which generic label we wish to attach to the play – if any – largely depends on how we interpret Ibsen's question-mark ending.

CHAPTER 3

TRANSLATING 'ET DUKKEHJEM'

Every generation needs its own translations of dramatic works, since drama, being intended for live, audiovisual presentation, must elicit immediate response from a mass audience. Words which have become obsolete and phrases which sound old-fashioned may well be accepted by the reader of drama, but for the spectator, who has little time to ponder, they will create a barrier. Plays which have reached a considerable age are therefore in greater need of new translations than novels – even if the target text with every new translation will tend to be further removed from the source text.

A second reason, applying to older works within both genres, is that many early translations are defective, partly because of imperfect or non-existent copyright laws and partly because of the undeveloped state of the art of translation.

A Doll's House is a case in point. Ibsen's Dano-Norwegian was somewhat different from today's Norwegian, which in its written form knows two varieties: the 'Bokmål' (Book Language), used by the majority of the population, and the 'Nynorsk' (New Norwegian), 'based on those modern dialects which most faithfully preserved the forms of Old Norwegian',[1] used by a minority. While Ibsen's Dano-Norwegian is very close to the Book Language, it is rather different from the New Norwegian. As a result we may speak of minor adaptations to present-day Book Language, mostly with regard to spelling, and of translations into New Norwegian.

With regard to the copyright problems, Ibsen's letter to *Nationaltidende*, dated Munich, 17 February 1880, is illuminating. There he states:

> As long as there is no literary convention in force between Germany
> and the Scandinavian countries, we Scandinavian authors are
> completely powerless down here, just as German authors are with
> us. Our dramatic works are therefore constantly exposed to violent
> treatment at the hands of translators and of theatre managements,
> of producers and of actors in the minor theatres.[2]

In some, notably older translations, censorship may have played a
part. But even in as late a rendering as that of Eva Le Galienne,[3] the
references to Nora's silk-stockings are omitted.

Ibsen was well aware of the harm a poor translation could do to
his work. At a banquet in Stockholm on 11 April 1898 he pointed to
the defectiveness of many target texts: 'What one reads in translation is … always in danger of being more or less misunderstood; for
translators are unfortunately all too often lacking in understanding.'[4] Referring to a production of *An Enemy of the People* at the
Royal Dramatic Theatre in Stockholm, he once told Swedish director August Lindberg:

> The translator misunderstood many places in the Norwegian text,
> and other parts were rendered poorly, in heavy, unnatural speech,
> and using expressions and turns of phrase that do not occur in
> ordinary Swedish speech. The dialogue must seem perfectly
> natural, and the manner of expression must differ from character
> to character.[5]

This criticism applies also to William Archer, although Ibsen's poor
command of English prevented him from forming a clear opinion of
Archer's renderings. For a long time the prime translator of Ibsen
into English, Archer lost his privileged position when new, more satisfying translations began to appear in the 1960s.

As already indicated, the most wide-spread modern British translation of *A Doll's House*, at least in the theatre, is the one provided by
Michael Meyer, who maintains that the play

> presents fewer problems to the translator than any other of Ibsen's
> plays, except perhaps *An Enemy of the People*. It is simply and directly
> written, and for nearly all the time the characters say what they
> mean, instead of talking at a tangent to their real meaning.[6]

Granted that many of the other plays may present even greater
translation problems, the idea that the characters in *A Doll's House*
'say what they mean' seems ill-founded. As we shall see, the play is
rather rich in passages evoking suggestive subtextual connotations.

Thomas Van Laan has examined the six translations of *A Doll's
House* 'that the English-speaking reader is most likely to come in
contact with'.[7] Why limit oneself to the reader when dealing with a
genre intended in the first place for the spectator? Since the difference in national idiom is especially important when we deal with
oral presentation, we may note that three of the translations selected
by Van Laan are British, three American. Just as British theatre-goers
wish to hear Ibsen's characters speak British English, so American
ones prefer to hear them communicate in American English.

Van Laan finds Archer often lacking in a sense of rhythm; Le
Galienne by far the worst of the translators; McFarlane sometimes
replacing Ibsen's suggestive metaphors by cliché expressions; Meyer
too loose in his rendering of the source text and at times insensitive
to stylistic registers; Reinert often failing to reproduce the characteristic phrasing of Ibsen's text; and Fjelde mistakenly substituting verbal variation for Ibsen's repetition of identical words. Fjelde's translation, Van Laan concludes, is 'the best of the six ... because it is the
most authentic', by which he means that the translator has succeeded in retaining 'not only the gist of the original but also its tone and
rhythms'.[8]

Rather than select a prize-winner on holistic grounds, we shall in
the following examine some of the problems involved in the translation of *A Doll's House*, especially problems that are generically determined, by focusing on how various translators have rendered the
same source text passages. The examples will be taken from four

translations, three British: McFarlane, Meyer, and Watts, one American: Fjelde.[9]

The most fundamental problem is connected with the fact that plays, unlike novels, are written for two kinds of recipients: readers and spectators. This has important consequences also for the way in which plays are translated. It is a well-known fact that literary oriented people often frown at translations used in the theatre, because they deviate too much from the source text. Conversely, directors and actors often find 'literary' translations awkward on the stage, sensing that they are unsuited both for oral and aural presentation. This being the situation, one may wonder whether we do not, in fact, need two kinds of drama translations, one for the reader, another for the spectator. A comparison between two such translations might tell us much about media differences and about the skill with which Ibsen, not least in *Et Dukkehjem*, has managed to direct himself to two kinds of recipients. For while this *can* be done reasonably well in a source text, it is exceedingly hard to do it in a target text. The playwright's dilemma is to an even greater extent that of his translator.

When read, a play may be compared to a novel. In both cases cultural signifiers that are unintelligible outside the source text area can be explained in notes. The situation becomes more problematic when a play is experienced by a spectator. In the theatre such signifiers will either remain unexplained or be explained by clarifying additions in the dialogue.

Traditionally, the English title of Ibsen's play is *A Doll's House*. When the leading American translator of Ibsen, Rolf Fjelde, prefers the title *A Doll House*, it is because the house is not Nora's; because the familiar children's toy is called 'a doll house'; and because 'one can make a reasonable supposition that Ibsen … at least partially includes Torvald with Nora in the original title *Et Dukkehjem*, for the two of them at the play's opening are still posing like the little marzipan bride and groom atop the wedding cake.'[10]

However, defenders of the traditional English title could object that the form 'doll's house' in Britain seems to be the normal one for the familiar children's toy; that only Nora is depicted as a doll in the play; that it is she who complains that both her father and, after him, Helmer have been treating her as a doll; and that the singular possessive in 'doll's house' does not automatically imply one possessor (compare the expression 'bird's nest').

A third alternative is offered by Errol Durbach who speaks of '*A Doll's House* when referring to the play and "the dolls' house" when dealing with the sociological phenomenon that is the play's subject – the world of middle-class values and assumptions'. But it is certainly odd to separate the play's title in this way from what according to Durbach is its basic theme. Besides, here again the plural form would rather relate to Nora and the Helmer children, who are explicitly referred to as her dolls, than to the idea that *all* the characters in the play are dolls, leading a life of 'mechanized domestic bliss'.[11] Extending the word to embrace all the characters means that the idea of appearance versus reality, that is central to the play, is replaced by the less natural idea of puppets pulled by unseen strings, that is, the idea of determinism.

What few translators seem to realise is that Ibsen's title 'does not mean a house for dolls, which in Norwegian is *dukkehus*, or *dukkestue*. Before Ibsen, *et dukkehjem* was a small, cozy, neat home; his play gave it the pejorative meaning.'[12] It is obvious that 'a doll house' no more than 'a doll's house' retains the connotations of the original. Rather than being superior to the traditional rendering, it simply sounds more idiomatic to Americans. The choice of target title will, in other words, depend on whether one has a British or an American audience in mind.

Another translation problem more directly relating to national differences is found in sequence 5. Whereas Meyer's characters speak of English money, those of McFarlane and Watts stick to the Norwegian monetary system. Watts even provides a footnote which informs us that 'fifty øre' is 'the equivalent of a sixpence', while 'a hundred øre equals one krone, then worth just over a shilling' – helpful information for the reader but not for the spectator; the latter runs the risk of missing the whole point of the money transaction.

An essential translation question is how to deal with significant correspondences. In *A Doll's House* the connection between Nora and the Christmas tree is even verbally present in the Norwegian original: in the beginning Nora speaks of the tree being 'pyntet' (decorated), while midway through the play Mrs Linde expresses her wish to see Nora 'pyntet'. This significant correspondence is – unavoidably? – lost in Meyer's rendering (emphasis added):

> NORA ... The children mustn't see it before I've *decorated* it.   (*seq.4*)
>
> MRS LINDE I did so want to see Nora *in her costume*.   (*seq.62*)

Once we see the significance of the Christmas tree, it makes a difference whether Nora herself is to decorate it – as Meyer has it – or whether the question of who is to do it is left open, as Ibsen, McFarlane and Watts have it.

A closer examination of the way in which the theme of guidance is handled in the source text and in two of the English translations, both from 1965, reveals a classic translation problem (emphasis added):

> NORA ... *vejled* mig, som du plejer.   (*seq.52*)
>
> NORA ... *lead* me, the way you always do.   (*Meyer*)
>
> NORA ... *show* me *where I'm wrong*, the way you always do.   (*Watts*)
>
> HELMER ... så kan jeg bedre *vejlede* hende.   (*seq.52*)
>
> HELMER ... Then it'll be easier for me to *show* her.   (*Meyer*)
>
> HELMER ... then I can *show* her better.   (*Watts*)
>
> HELMER Nå, her må rigtignok *vejledning* til.
>
> NORA ... Du må *vejlede* mig lige til det sidste.   (*seq.53*)
>
> HELMER I'll have to *show* you every step.

NORA ... You must *show* me every step of the way. Right to the end of the dance. (*Meyer*)

HELMER Well, you certainly need a lot of *coaching*.

NORA ... You must *coach* me up to the last minute. (*Watts*)

Ibsen here uses the word 'vejlede' (guide) three times and the corresponding noun 'vejledning' (guidance) once. Toward the end of the play Helmer declares himself prepared to 'vejlede' the erring Nora with the help of another 'usvikelig vejleder' (infallible guide): religion. The meaning of the term has become greatly extended. It is precisely through these repetitions of the same root in different contexts that we are made aware of the significant correspondence between guidance in dance (Act II) and guidance in life (Act III).

Turning to the translations we discover that neither Meyer nor Watts retains Ibsen's consistency of vocabulary here. As a result, the correspondence between the guidance offered in Act II and the one offered in Act III is obscured. Ibsen's three-word phrase 'til det sidste' (up to the end) is rendered as 'every step of the way. Right to the end of the dance' by Meyer and as 'up to the last minute' by Watts. The delicate, ironical balance in Ibsen's text between a literal level (Helmer) and a figurative one (Nora), *not understood by him*, is disturbed in Meyer's wordy, explicatory rendering. The metaphorical significance of the dance guidance has become too explicit.

The most striking key words in the play are the adjective 'vidunderlig' and the corresponding noun 'det vidunderlige', the latter variously translated as 'the wonderful', 'the wonderful thing', 'the miracle', and 'something miraculous'. The two words, mentioned no less than nineteen times, are, as Ibsen himself notes, constantly linked with Nora.[13] And they are almost untranslatable, even into languages closely related to Norwegian. For the Swedish première Ibsen suggested that 'det vidunderlige' should be rendered as 'det underbara', literally 'the wonderful'. This, however, sounds rather commonplace, and in his recent production Ingmar Bergman characteristically preferred the somewhat strange-sounding 'det vidunderliga'.

The choice of target expression here seems closely linked to the question whether or not one considers Nora's ideal possible to realise.

A closer inspection of the text reveals that Nora moves from a fairly everyday use of 'vidunderlig' to the more mystifying 'det vidunderlige', and from there to the climactic substantival superlative 'det vidunderligste' (the most wonderful thing) that has a fairy-talish ring. Along with Helmer we wonder what the most wonderful thing can be. Since Nora's closing line – 'That our life together could become a marriage.' – apparently provides the answer to this question; 'det vidunderligste' – the existence of which Nora has come to doubt! – can be identified as 'a true marriage'. By a true marriage Nora obviously means a relationship in which husband and wife love one another so much that they are prepared to sacrifice themselves for each other. Nora's view of Helmer, before her eyes are opened to his real nature, is based on the Christian idea of *satisfactio vicaria*.[14] Believing, or wishing to believe, that once Helmer hears of her forgery, he will take the blame for it, she applies what she has learned from clergyman Hansen about Jesus to her own husband. Ironically, it is not the 'idealistic' Nora and Helmer but the realistic Mrs Linde and Krogstad who, now ready for a true marriage, experience, if not 'det vidunderligste', at least a realistic counterpart of it.

Although there are no good equivalents for 'det vidunderlige' in English, it is important that the playwright's insistence on the same word, in its various inflections, be retained. For how else can we sense its importance to Nora? Yet

> Although Ibsen's Nora, in the space of two brief speeches, speaks three times of the coming or not of 'det vidunderlige,' using the same two words each time … Fjelde gives us 'the miraculous thing,' 'miracles,' and 'the miraculous event.'[15]

Variation here counteracts the idea that Nora is constantly concerned with one and the same miracle, that of a true marriage. At the same time Nora's climactic ending with a substantival superlative makes the words 'miracle' and 'miraculous' unsuitable, since they are absolutes defying inflection.

Much of the significance of the dialogue between Rank and Nora depends on *double-entendres*, some of which do not carry over into English. When Rank in Act III, about to leave the Helmers, asks for a cigar and Nora, striking a match, lights it, her gesture may well be suggestive to us, but the target dialogue – 'Let me give you light' – hardly adds any meaning to it. When he leaves, the Rank of the target language says to Nora: 'Sleep well. And thanks for the light.' Nora and the recipient at this point share two secrets about Rank, both of them hidden to Helmer: Rank's love for Nora and his proximity to death. As a result we interpret the quoted lines, not literally and trivially as Helmer does, but metaphorically as Nora and Rank do. While the *double-entendre* is carried over in the translations with regard to Rank's 'Sleep well', it is more or less lost in the reference to Nora's handing Rank 'light' rather than, as Ibsen has it, 'ild' (fire), a word with obvious erotic connotations. Knowing at this point that she will never see Rank again, Ibsen's Nora dares to respond to his earlier declaration of love. And Rank thanks her for it. The significance of this exchange between them, centering around that little word 'ild', is necessarily lost in English translation. It is questionable whether Nora's and Rank's verbal *double-entendre* in a performance can be retained by non-verbal means (gestures, glances) without their letting Helmer in on their mutual secrets.

The transference from source to target language necessarily gives rise to new verbal constellations. Usually this means that significant word patterns in the source text are obscured or disappear altogether. But once in a while the process is reversed:

HELMER ... Har du klædt dig om?

NORA (*i sin hverdagskjole*) Ja, Torvald, nu har jeg klædt mig om.

(*seq. 73*)

HELMER ... Have you changed?

    NORA (*in her everyday dress*) Yes, Torvald, I've changed. (*Meyer*)

HELMER ... You've changed your dress?

    NORA Yes, Torvald, I've changed my dress. (*Fjelde*)

In Fjelde's rather literal rendering of Ibsen's dialogue – and omission of his acting-direction! – the deeper significance of Nora's change of dress is obscured, while Meyer's laconic one is actually an improvement on Ibsen. For while the playwright later (seq. 76) has Nora claim that she and her husband would have to 'forvandle os således at – ', by Fjelde rendered as 'You and I both would have to transform ourselves to the point that – ', Meyer translates the passage: 'You and I would both have to change so much that – '. Unlike Ibsen and Fjelde, Meyer suggestively links the changing of the dress with the change of mind.

The most succinct contrasting of the sexes is found in the following frequently quoted exchange between husband and wife:

HELMER Der er ingen, som ofrer sin *ære* for den man elsker.

    NORA Det har hundrede tusend kvinder gjort. (*seq. 74*)

HELMER But nobody sacrifices his *honour* for the one he loves.

    NORA Hundreds of thousands of women have. (*McFarlane*)

HELMER But no man can be expected to sacrifice his honour, even for the person he loves.

    NORA Millions of women have done it. (*Meyer*)

HELMER But no man would sacrifice his *honour* for the one he loves.

    NORA Thousands of women have. (*Watts*)

HELMER But there's no one who gives up honor for love.

    NORA Millions of women have done just that. (*Fjelde*)

In this famous repartee the ethics of the two genders are strongly contrasted. But the irony of Helmer's line is that, generalising from his male morals, he speaks of 'ingen' (nobody), not of 'ingen mand', as one would assume from Meyer's and Watts' rendering (no man).

Ibsen's Nora speaks of exactly a hundred thousand women. McFarlane increases it to 'hundreds of thousands', Meyer and Fjelde to 'millions', while Watts strangely limits it to 'thousands'. Evidently the translators have found the exactness of Ibsen's figure disturbing. And most of them have found it too low to make any impression. Presumably the large populations of Britain and America, as compared to Norway, have determined the increased numbers. We may also note that Helmer's emphasis of *ere* is a paralinguistic acting-direction not indicated by two of the translators.

A somewhat special problem is found in Nora's last, exceedingly important speech. In the original the relevant passage reads:

NORA ... Å, Torvald, jeg tror ikke længer på noget vidunderligt.
HELMER Men jeg vil tro på det. Nævn det! Forvandle os således at – ?
NORA At samliv mellem os to kunde bli'e et ægteskab. Farvel. (*seq. 76*)

Since drama translations play an important role not least with regard to paralinguistics – for instance, diction, emphasis, tempo – it is interesting to see how this passage has been rendered by the four translators:

NORA ... Oh, Torvald, I don't believe in miracles any more.
HELMER But I *will* believe. Name it! Change to the point where ...
NORA Where we could make a real marriage of our lives together. Goodbye! (*McFarlane*)

NORA ... oh, Torvald, I don't believe in miracles any longer.
HELMER But I want to believe in them. Tell me. We should have to change so much that – !
NORA That life together between us two could become a marriage. Goodbye. (*Meyer*)

NORA ... Oh, Torvald, I don't believe in miracles any longer.
HELMER But I'll believe. Tell me: 'so changed that ...'?
NORA That our life together could be a real marriage. Good-bye. (*Watts*)

NORA ... Oh, Torvald, I've stopped believing in miracles.

HELMER But I'll believe. Tell me! Transform ourselves to the point that ...?

NORA That our living together could be a true marriage. (*Fjelde*)

Although the differences may seem small, they are of significance to the actor and actress playing the parts of Helmer and Nora. Ibsen speaks of *one* miracle – or, rather, of something wonderful – the translators, for idiomatic reasons, of several. While Helmer's first sentence in the original is somewhat circumstantial, giving the actor a variety of possibilities as to how to phrase it, it is much shorter with Watts and Fjelde. McFarlane provides an implicit paralinguistic signifier, alien to the source text, by having Helmer emphasise his willingness to believe. Fjelde omits the final 'Goodbye', perhaps out of a feeling that Nora's pungent key line should not be followed by anything at all. Yet by doing so, he is not only deviating from his own dictum that 'it is the translator's job to convey ... the whole text'.[16] He is actually 'directing' the ending. For if the word does not appear in the target text, the actress playing Nora will be more inclined to exclude the possibility that her leave-taking is a friendly one.

Nora's final speech is, in a sense, culture-bound. When Ibsen penned it, the word marriage had very positive connotations – especially in the playwright's Dano-Norwegian tongue, since the noun 'ægteskab' (marriage) would suggest that the relationship is 'ægte' (genuine, honest). The word 'samliv' (life together) presumably sounded more neutral or even slightly pejorative. A century later the relations between the sexes have changed so much that 'marriage' to many has lost its positive value, while 'life together' in the era of unmarried cohabitation has become more respectable. This semantic shift means that present-day directors are faced with a problem: if you want to make Nora's final speech meaningful to a modern audience, you are forced to change Ibsen's phrasing of it. What a director here *should* do, a translator must certainly not do.

Nora sees 'life together' and 'marriage' as two different things which should be integrated, fused. Although legally sanctioned, Nora's and Helmer's relationship has in fact, she now discovers, never existed in any deeper sense. What she means by 'ægteskab' is a true marriage, a physical and spiritual relationship based on equality and mutual respect. However, by referring not to 'et sant ægteskab' (a true marriage) but simply to 'et ægteskab' (a marriage), Nora reveals that no other form of marriage is valid to her. Just as in the case of the forgery, she is indifferent to outward manifestations and concerned only with the inner meaning. It is therefore hardly true to the spirit of the speech to translate 'ægteskab' with 'a real' or 'a true' marriage. As for 'samliv', it is impossible to find an exact equivalent for this concept in English, and the terseness of Nora's speech is necessarily lost in translation. Of the variants offered, 'our life together' suggests a more intimate, more traditional conjugal situation than 'our lives together', where a greater amount of independence within the marriage is indicated. 'Life together between us' seems a clumsily literal rendering, whereas 'our living together' sounds somewhat prosaic.

Let me conclude this brief survey of translation problems on a hilarious note by adding to the four solutions just quoted the one provided by the very first English translation of the play. In the rendering of the Dane T. Weber, published in 1880, Nora's final speech reads: 'That cohabitation between you and me might become a matrimony.'[17] Whatever weak spots may still be found in recent target versions of *Et Dukkehjem*, there is no doubt that considerable progress has been made in the art of translating Ibsen's play since schoolmaster Weber tried his hand at it.

CHAPTER 4

'A DOLL'S HOUSE' AS STAGE PLAY

Since few plays have been as widely performed as *A Doll's House*, the following survey can merely provide limited information about some of the more remarkable productions.[1] Practically all the information is based on impressions by observers of the various productions, mostly reviewers. Their descriptions contain the usual lacunae. We hear quite a lot about such topics as directorial 'message', role interpretation, and stage design, but very little about the less durative elements of a performance: lighting, proxemics, kinesics, mimicry, paralinguistics.

Possibly the most frequently produced of all of Ibsen's plays – *Ghosts* and *Hedda Gabler* would be the closest rivals – there is little to support the sometimes heard view that *A Doll's House* is dated. In many countries the first Ibsen play to reach the stage, it has in most of them been revived from time to time. In the Netherlands, to pick a random example, the play has to date experienced twenty-four professional productions, seven of which were staged by foreign guest companies.[2]

The world première took place at the Royal Theatre in Copenhagen on 21 December 1879 – a season and year agreeing well with that in the play. Two weeks earlier the drama had been published.[3] The critics thus had a chance to read the text before they reviewed the production. We may safely assume that their views of the performance were partly based on their impressions of the play text – as is usually the case with critics. Conversely, those who start by witnessing a production would naturally have it at the back of their minds when reading the play afterwards. Betty Hennings,

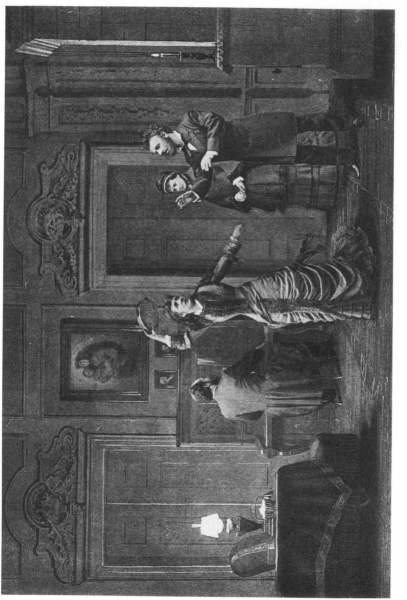

1 The first Nora: Betty Hennings dancing the tarantella at the 1879 world première, directed by H. P. Holst, at the Royal Theatre, Copenhagen.

Herman Bang writes, transformed 'even readers to spectators because, after we have but once seen her, she follows us from scene to scene, we see her and not Nora, even as we read'.[4]

The quality of any theatre production is likely to depend, in part, on the length of the rehearsal period. With no director in the modern sense and only eleven rehearsals preceding it, the original 1879 production was nevertheless a success. Although we now expect much longer rehearsal periods, there may still be considerable variation. Being used to rehearsing for some two months in Norway, Liv Ullmann found it difficult to accept a mere three weeks for the New York 1975 production. Especially since English is not her native tongue.[5]

Ironically, the first stage productions of the play in English, in Milwaukee 1882 and London 1884, were adaptations, the first one entitled *The Child Wife*, the second *Breaking a Butterfly*. In *The Child Wife*, 'an Irish widow was introduced to provide some humor', while 'in the second act one of Nora's children sang a solo'.[6] In *Breaking a Butterfly* Ibsen's play was parodically ridiculed.

Even when treated respectfully, the play has frequently been cut and/or adapted. But the reasons for this and the manner in which it has been done have, of course, been widely different. In the 1893 London guest performance Eleonora Duse acted 'in a heavily cut Italian text'. As is often the case, the sequence with the children was omitted, presumably for practical reasons. Bringing Italian child actors on tour would have been a problem. Besides, as a critic pointed out in connection with the 1962 Stockholm performance, 'it is difficult to get children to act in a spontaneously happy way on the stage'.[7]

In puritanic America, omissions served to make the play more respectable. For the 1894 New York performance, Nora's references to her stockings were eliminated and Dr Rank's discussion of his disease was limited to one sentence.[8]

While the early productions indicate how hard it was for Ibsen's contemporaries to accept the play – especially the ending – as written, later adaptations have usually been motivated by a wish to bring it closer to a modern audience. The changes here range from the deletion of a few lines to a drastic slimming down of the text, as in the case of Ingmar Bergman.

Peter Zadek's 1967 Bremen production, on the eve of the student revolt, was not surprisingly conceived in Brechtian terms. The director

> not only repudiated the conventions of realistic illusion and atmospherics but also rearranged the text itself in epic manner, as a succession of clearly profiled individual scenes marked off from one another by blackouts that emphasized a sense of discontinuity and montage.[9]

In the Stockholm 1978 version, Jan Håkanson inserted some passages from the draft of the play, notably Nora's key statement that she has 'more faces than one'. In order to make Helmer less ridiculous and more human, he also cleared the text of some of Helmer's self-righteous remarks.[10] The performance opened with a directorial addition: the Helmer family gathering for a group photograph. A *tableau vivant* showing the social façade that is presented to the world, the family group was later retained as a projection on the curtain.

As might be expected, the realistic setting in the original 1879 production was characterised by fidelity to Ibsen's stage-directions. But there were some additions: 'flowering plants, floral bouquets, and chairs with flowered seat-covers', all of which 'conveyed an air of middle-class refinement in the Helmer household'.[11] Among the books in expensive bindings prescribed by the playwright, a bust of Venus could be seen, while a reproduction of Raphael's *Madonna with Child* was given a prominent place above the piano. By these visual signifiers the director departed from Ibsen and from the very beginning indicated Helmer's adherence to Nora's socially determined triple role of sexual object, 'virgin' and mother.

In the Christiania 1880 production, William Archer complained, 'the scene . . . was not really well set – a heavy red-papered room, by no means the fine light *dagligstue* of the Helmers'.[12] However, Ibsen never prescribes, as Archer implies, that the living-room should be kept in light colours. Instead of a *Madonna with Child*, a landscape was here hung above the piano, presenting a rather vacant signifier.

In the London 1889 version the tiled stove, the prints by Thorvaldsen on the walls and, especially, a newspaper on the couch helped to suggest the Norwegian location,[13] while the Parisians five years later were offered a rather strange idea of what the home of a Norwegian bank-manager would look like: 'a gaunt and arras-hung baronial hall, decked with trophies of war and of the chase – as though the Helmers had taken a flat in the Castle of Otranto!'[14]

Very different and much more sensible is the view of the setting we come across in a letter to Meyerhold from Vera Kommisarjevskaya, who played the part of Nora both in the 1904 and in the 1906 St Petersburg productions. For the living-room, she writes,

> a very warm, cozy, and pleasant nest, isolated from the *real* world, must be created . . . We will change the color and texture of the materials. We will lay a new carpet (so the sound of steps is not heard). We will replace the chairs with something comfortable and low. From one side a red glow from the fireplace must be seen in the last act, so Linde and Krogstad are not obliged to play their scene by moonlight.[15]

But Meyerhold did not share these views. In his 1906 production the spectators were confronted with a stylised, cool and unattractive set: a cramped passageway with a decrepit piano in one corner, a 'dilapidated three-legged table, two inconspicuous chairs, an arbitrarily suspended window flanked by ballooning, and cranberry-coloured drapes that reached the full height of the stage'.[16] Meyerhold's setting, the Markers conclude, seemed 'in *deliberate* contradiction of what the characters *say*'.

A similar, radical departure from idyllic realism characterised the setting of the 1922 Moscow production:

> The setting used old decorations turned inside-out, parts of pavilions, gridiron guide bars, etc. Thus, the stage gave the

> impression that everything was collapsing, everything was going
> to the devil, down and out . . . Against this background the phrase
> of the self-satisfied bourgeois, Helmer: 'It's nice here, Nora, cozy,'
> could not evoke a tempestuous reaction from the auditorium.[17]

Some directors have relocated the play in time, if not in place. The
1929 Oslo production, apparently in an attempt to suggest the relevance of the play for different generations, presented 'furniture and
costumes from the past fifty years',[18] while the 1936 Copenhagen
version settled for 'a handsome modern room in which the characters walked about like everyday modern people'. The problem with
such an updating of the play, Frederik Schyberg pointed out, is that
Nora is turned into 'a modern young woman wrestling in full seriousness with problems and ideas that have been talked out by everyone else almost two generations ago'. Instead of being modernised,
the play, he argued, becomes antiquated theatre. 'Paradoxical as it
may sound', the critic summarised, only when they are performed in
historical costume, are Ibsen's plays 'lifted above all dependency on
period'.[19]

Stately realism was applied in the 1936 Oslo setting, showing 'the
palm in the window, the green upholstered mahogany furniture, the
pompous white tile stove standing on the floor, and the hallway with
its huge panes of glass looking out on one of those hopelessly "elegant" staircases from the eighties.'[20] In the London production of
the same year the stuffiness of the unattractive living-room, which
showed great fidelity to the period, overpowered the characters on
the stage.[21] Three years later the Londoners were introduced to 'the
amazing architecture of Torvald's summer palace', seemingly relocated to 'the ground floor of Park Lane's latest and most luxurious
blocks of flats'.[22] For the 1953 London production, directed by Peter
Ashmore, the stage designer 'provided a multiple set that opened up
the entire living area of the Helmer household – including the master bedroom'.[23]

A more traditional solution characterised the 1962 Stockholm
interior, where the idyllic living-room in blue and yellow – the

2 Helmer (Mogens Wieth) relaxing after Krogstad's second letter, whereas Nora (Mai Zetterling), already stripped of her masquerade costume, turns her back on him. From Peter Ashmore's 1953 production at the Lyric Theatre, Hammersmith.

Swedish national colours – was emphatically presented as the room of a doll's house. To one critic this cosy interior seemed ironically appropriate as background for 'the most famous of all family settlements',[24] while another found it too light and airy to provide the proper feeling of imprisoning patriarchy.[25] Ten years later the

Stockholmers were again invited, in the same theatre, to a cosy, bourgeois, somewhat frugal interior, indicative of the fact that the Helmers are still waiting for the money to come in.[26] Even further in this direction was the 1992 London production, where 'the simple, almost shabby furniture' suggested 'that the Helmers have only just come out of the economic straits'.[27]

In Peter Zadek's wilful 1967 Bremen production the spectator was faced with an exceedingly empty room, in fact hardly recognisable as a room: 'a door on either side, a veranda window as background, an old-fashioned sofa at the diagonal mid-point of the stage, and virtually nothing more'.[28]

For the 1974 Oslo production Arne Walentin had designed a sparsely furnished living-room enclosed by red-brown walls with a pattern of white roses so prominent that it irritated Aud Thagaard.[29] Through the hall you could see the door with the fatal letter-box.

Jürgen Rose's stage design for the 1976 Berlin production faithfully reflected the director's, Rudolf Noelte's, 'staunch belief in the importance of a recognizable environment in the performance of Ibsen's prose plays'.[30]

In the 1978 Stockholm production, the claustrophobic effect of Ibsen's setting was undermined by the fact that Helmer's study and the dining-room could be glimpsed behind the attractive, green-tinted living-room, while in the 1986 Stratford production by the Royal Shakespeare Company, the scenographer, Kit Surrey, although departing from Ibsen's realistic interior, retained much of its implicit significance:

> The carpet emphasized the doors and gave the set a feeling of being surrounded by other rooms – not only in the apartment itself, but also in the rest of the building. Privacy in this environment is at a premium . . . The couple take great pains not to disturb their neighbours . . .
>
> On this brown carpet, Kit Surrey placed furniture and effects carefully chosen to signal the status and image that this couple wish to present to the world and to themselves.[31]

3 The Helmer living-room as recreated by Arne Walentin in the 1974 production, directed by Pål Skjønsberg and Elisabeth Bang, at the Norwegian Theatre in Oslo.

In the 1985 Gothenburg production the scene designer had built a doll's house of sorts on the stage and had the characters appear on a raised platform,[32] indications that the setting was related to the theatrical possibilities inherent in the text. The walls of the living-room were merely indicated; behind them a winter landscape could be seen with the Helmer children throwing snowballs at one another – in anticipation of the conflict between their parents. Once the lights were transferred to the interior, the warm orange-red carpet of the room contrasted vividly with the bluish cold outside.

As indicated earlier, the age of the characters is not merely something determined by plausibility. It also helps to describe them and, especially, the relations between them. A marriage between two people of about the same age obviously makes a different impression to one in which the husband is considerably older than his wife – not to mention the opposite possibility, which might well seem disturbing in a serious performance of *A Doll's House*.

While the reader of the play is free to give the characters the age that seems most reasonable to him or her, the spectator is forced to accept what actors and actresses offer him. And that means a great deal of variation from one production to another. Of special importance is, of course, the age of the protagonist, Nora;

> Nazimova first played the part of Nora, when she was 28, Minnie
> Maddern Fiske when she was 29 . . . but both continued to play her
> until they were almost 40. When Vera Kommisarzhevskaya first
> performed the role in St Petersburg, she was in her late thirties;
> when she performed in New York, she was 44. Janet Achurch
> startled London by performing the role in 1889; she was then 35.
> When she was 49, it was still in her repertory, for which reason Shaw
> urged her to drop it. . . . Modjeska was 28 when she acted Nora;
> Ruth Gordon was 41. Jane Fonda was 37 and Claire Bloom 40. . . .
> Liv Ullmann was 35 when she played Nora in New York, but even in
> person she looks 10 years younger. At 34, Julie Harris performed the
> role in so convincingly girlish a manner that she did not seem two
> years older than Christopher Plummer, which she is.[33]

To this list we may add that the first Nora, the Danish Betty Hennings, was twenty-nine when she first did the part and no less than fifty-seven when she did it for the last time,[34] whereas the Swedish Harriet Bosse was nearly fifty, also far beyond the lark-and-squirrel age. The Norwegian Tore Segelcke was a youthful Nora in 1936, 'but when she reappeared in the play opposite a much younger Helmer twelve years later, the vulnerability became even more poignant'.[35] Bibi Andersson gave the impression of being a relatively young Nora married to a man (Bengt Virdestam) of about the same age. 'A young couple', one critic commented, 'who at least have a common source of joy in sexuality.'[36]

Nora is the hub around which everything turns. It is therefore not surprising that this part has always been relished by actresses. As Janet Achurch, one of the early Noras, put it:

> It is the hardest part I have ever played. Nora is never off the stage for a single moment during the whole of the first and second acts, and in the third act she is only absent for five minutes. . . . I like Nora better than about 200 roles I have filled since I first appeared on the stage.[37]

How is one to play Nora? There is of course no single answer to this question. The time and place of the performance, the director's intentions, the kind of actress doing the part and many other circumstances are of great relevance here. In the case of Vera Kommisarjevskaya (New York 1908) we may even speak of a definite acting style: 'Her acting was particularly remarkable for its reserve and restraint; she was free from all theatrical tricks . . . I have never seen either on or off the stage a woman of more quiet dignity.'[38] As her brother Theodore, himself a successful director, explained, Kommisarjevskaya 'was very economical and synthetic in her mode of expression and avoided outward typical details. She insisted that an actor's means of expression should be restricted to the simplest fundamentals in order to show the essential inner life of a character.'[39]

The most crucial problem in any production of *A Doll's House* is how to handle Nora's transformation. The reviewers of the original 1879 production all agreed that the metamorphosis Ibsen's Nora undergoes in the third act seems utterly implausible. Yet, judging by the reviews, the implausibility is not so immersed in the text that it cannot be overcome in performance. Most commentators praised Betty Hennings 'for her handling of this undeniably difficult transition from songbird to new woman'.[40] But Ove Rode disagreed. To him Mrs Henning's Nora 'fell into two parts, both equally striking in performance. But the gay little squirrel held not the slightest hint of that Nora whose terror later rouses her to seriousness.'[41] To Maurice Baring, on the other hand, who saw the actress in a production many years later, Betty Hennings 'made the transformation, which whenever I had seen the play before seemed so difficult to believe in, of the Nora of the first act into the Nora of the last act, seem the most natural thing in the world.'[42] However, by that time Mrs Hennings had 'changed her interpretation completely; she was able to penetrate more deeply into the soul of the woman who was at once so childishly unaware of life and yet so brave before the unknown . . .'[43]

A similar, age-determined reinterpretation of the part applies to the famous Johanne Dybwad:

> In 1890 at Christiania Theatre she was young herself, and her Nora was little more than a child, the happy 'lark' girl who could not quite fathom the new reality; sixteen years later at the National Theatre she was a woman who hid a secret fear of life and whose sudden insight into terrors forced her thoughts into strange paths.[44]

Commenting on the latter production, Axel Otto Normann did not believe in Dybwad's transformation: 'it seemed to me as though there was a breach in the character, I missed a clear and convincing transition from the first to the last two acts'.[45]

Similarly, we learn that the Norwegian Harriet Bosse, once Strindberg's third wife, in the Stockholm production of 1925 'did not in the last act manage to transform the poor little doll Nora into a woman'.[46] According to Georg Nordensvan, 'she did not believe in the final act herself'.[47] What is here seen as a flaw *could* of course be seen as a way of making the role consistent – at the expense of the 'message' of the play. Like Bosse, Ruth Gordon (New York 1937) failed to become the new woman. Instead of changing the mood, she continued 'as chirrupy as a sparrow'.[48] A similar kind of criticism was directed against Bibi Andersson's Nora (Stockholm 1972): 'the softness of her acting and diction make this ideal Nora too ideal – the tension ceases, the revolt pales, and the immutable logic of the liberation loses much of its sharpness'.[49]

By contrast, Ove Rode claimed that Johanne Juell (Christiania 1880) was 'the first to hold Nora's character together, so that the childish gaiety of the first act did not clash incomprehensibly and crudely with the mature seriousness that follows the catastrophe'.[50] Similarly, Ida Ålberg (Helsinki 1880), according to Gerhard Gran, 'did not fall apart into two halves and it never occurred to us that it was not the same creature who crept on all fours and barked at her children in the first act, and in the last sat there as a responsible woman'.[51]

If we may believe these commentators, Agnes Sorma (Berlin 1894), who to Siegfrid Jacobsohn seemed 'the first to heal the Nora split',[52] was in fact not the first actress to manage this difficult task. Fourteen years later another Nora was to repeat this achievement. According to Phelps,

> altogether the most impressive [Ibsen] production was that given in America and in the Russian language by Madame Kommisarjevskaya, the only actress who completely convinced me that the Nora of the last act had naturally developed out of the 'little squirrel' of the first.[53]

From these statements we may conclude that only rarely have actresses managed to depict Nora's transformation in a convincing way. The part has in this respect always been a tremendous challenge.

Rather than show a Nora who develops from doll to mature woman, Kommisarjevskaya played a Nora who 'lives two lives – one visible, the other hidden. In her visible life, the Nora of Kommisarjevskaya remained unchanged . . . but in her hidden life she grows, acquires courage, and begins to grasp what she has never understood.'[54] Similarly, with Irene Triesch (Berlin 1906), 'the dramatic development seems to be not a process of growth and maturation, but rather one of release from a latent, already existing condition; not an evolution but an awakening of a human being from a strange bondage'.[55] According to Koht, Tore Segelcke (Oslo 1936) was the only Nora he had seen who made it clear already in Act I that she was merely acting the part Helmer required.[56] Kristian Elster, too, felt that Segelcke played the part as though she had 'seen through Helmer and herself and her doll-marriage long ago' and yet – or perhaps therefore – 'clings in desperation to this dream of the wonderful thing'.[57] Lydia Lopokova (London 1936), similarly, 'gave a convincing delineation of a Nora already conscious of her own nagging unhappiness from the outset'.[58] Gunn Wållgren (Stockholm 1962), interpreting the part in much the same way and merely pretended that she was a toy: 'The thoughtlessness and the naivety [were] not inherent in her but education and pose: a protective disguise that was removed as easily as the used-up tarantella costume.'[59] Again, Claire Bloom (London 1972) 'suggested early in the performance that Nora had courage and resources, and that her chirpy innocence was merely a pose'.[60]

Let me finish this brief exposé of some of the stage Noras with Liv Ullmann's (Oslo 1974, New York 1975) comments on her own interpretation of the role:

> This woman, who uses and manipulates those around her while at the same time wanting to help and love them, refuses to do something she feels is morally repugnant to her when the decisive moment comes. It is beyond her imagination to conceive of exploiting the situation when Dr Rank declares his love and begs to give her the money she so badly needs. . . . When she finally *sees*, she also understands that the anger she feels over everything that is false

4 Liv Ullmann as a worried Nora by the Christmas tree in Act II
of the 1974 production at the Norwegian Theatre, Oslo.

between them is directed just as much against herself as against him. Her responsibility was as great as his. She hopes that the change will also take place in him – not for her sake but for his own. . . . In the first acts Nora is not just the songbird and the squirrel; neither is she pure wisdom and feminine strength in the last.[61]

It will be seen from these comments that unlike earlier actresses who took Nora's naivety to be genuine and as a result had to make it credible to the audience that she undergoes an inner maturation in three days, later ones have been more inclined to see her naivety in the first two acts as a pose that she drops at the end, where she unmasks herself and shows Helmer – and us – her true face.

The divergent interpretations reflect a general change from a view of a homogeneous human psyche to a dualistic view, assuming that our conscious will is constantly in conflict with our unconscious drives. Applied to Nora, the latter view certainly appears more convincing to present-day audiences. Although Helmer's reaction to Krogstad's first letter is a painful revelation to her, this need not mean that it comes as a complete surprise to her. The revelation, we may assume, consists in the fact that the discrepancy between the miracle Nora has been hoping for – with diminishing conviction – and the stark reality is even greater than she could ever imagine.

Nora's transformation is visibly indicated by her exchanging her 'masquerade costume' for her '*everyday dress*', the significance of which is underlined by Nora's remark: 'Now I've changed my dress.' Ibsen thought of Nora's everyday costume as being 'a simple, blue woollen dress',[62] three adjectives indicating above all one thing: honesty. But since he does not in the play text specify what the everyday dress looks like, he apparently wanted to give directors a free hand in this matter. More important than the colour, material and cut of Nora's everyday dress is whether or not we have seen it earlier in the play. Many directors choose to let Nora appear in the same dress she has worn in the first two acts. But in this way her transformation is obscured, since the costume suitable for Nora as a doll is hardly a fitting one for Nora as a grown-up.

Ibsen's comment has led some directors to settle for a blue everyday dress. In the Malmö 1952 production Gertrud Fridh's Nora appeared in a 'light-blue walking dress', while Liv Ullmann's 1974 Nora was dressed more elegantly in blue velvet with laces and, in addition, a blue, fur-lined coat.

When the play is updated to correspond with the year of production, the costumes will, superficially, increase the possibilities of the audience identifying with the characters. Or they may increase the topical strength of the statement the director wants to make. In the 1905 New York production, which emphasised the contemporaneity of the situation, Ethel Barrymore

> wore the appropriate clothes of a modern young lady of the early twentieth century . . . in the first scene . . . . For the tarantella she chose harem pants with their evocative overtones of the bloomers so closely identified with the feminist cause. And when this Nora flounced out of the house, she had changed to a Norfolk jacket, an Oxford tie, and a short skirt, a costume that boldly suggested an association with the New Woman.[63]

If Nora's 'transformation' presents a problem, so does Helmer's caricaturist behaviour. In his review of the 1974 Oslo production, Odd Eidem pointed to the danger of weakening Helmer's part:

> If the performance as a whole is to be saved, one needs the right man to do Helmer . . . the play must be directed in such a way that Helmer is provided with enough brutal power to manage the few moments of victory he is given in the text. If he is forced to act quietly and too modestly . . . the power struggle will meaninglessly be in Nora's favour.[64]

A rather different and to my mind more convincing view has been expressed by Evert Sprinchorn.[65] Ibsen, he argues, was forced to make Helmer an authoritarian prig to motivate Nora's decision to leave him. Nowadays, when we can more easily accept Nora's choice, it is dangerous to present Helmer in this way, since the issue would be blurred by the fact that she is leaving a man who is no longer a representative husband. Consequently, there is every reason to tone down the more ridiculous aspects of Helmer to make him a worthy match for her and thereby retain something of the provocative power of the ending. In the words of another critic: 'If in the 1980s you do Helmer the way Ibsen shaped him with regard to the 1880s, you make yourself more immune to the situation in the theatre than was the play when written.'[66]

Opinions were, in fact, rather divided about the nature of the first Helmer (Emil Poulsen). To *Dags-Telegrafen* he seemed 'such a congenial, refined, professionally energetic and honest, domestically happy and likeable personality'.[67] *Berlingske Tidende* found that he nourished a deep and sincere love for Nora,[68] whereas *Fædrelandet* and Herman Bang saw him as a callous egoist. Poulsen's wish 'to prepare from the outset for the brutality which is one of the determining features in Helmer's character', Bang found, was utterly misplaced. The actor, he claimed, would have achieved more if he had initially portrayed Helmer as seemingly noble and refined.[69] Lasse Segelcke's Helmer (Oslo 1936), one critic assured, was up to the last act 'almost likeable'. Sam Waterston (New York 1975), the *Detroit News* reported, similarly 'allowed kindness to break through his exterior'. His softening the role made Helmer seem more trapped by the end of the play, and 'more unfortunate than Nora, who at least is trying to break out of her imprisoning role'.[70] Leif Ahrle's Helmer (Stockholm 1978) was 'a very intelligible and deplorable person' who made it credible that he had indeed loved his Nora in a deeper sense. Like Nora, he was 'a victim of a social system'.[71]

As these examples indicate, there is a marked tendency in more recent productions to make Helmer not a representative of a suppressing male society but its victim, as trapped in his male role as Nora is in her female one. This interpretation clearly reflects a changed attitude to bourgeois society, especially in the 1970s, the heyday of Marxism among western intellectuals.

Like Helmer, Krogstad has undergone a humanising process. A stock stage villain in many early presentations, he is nowadays usually seen more as a victim of social injustice and is consequently portrayed with considerable sympathy.

Sympathy has always been bestowed on Rank whose syphilis, far from being self-imposed, is the result of his father's lascivious life and thus, obliquely, of the double morals of society. A certain doubt was cast both on Nora and on Rank in the 1985 Gothenburg performance, where their intimacy seemed to indicate an erotic relation. For a moment, one critic wrote, the wild idea arises that Nora has been infected by Rank.[72]

Kristine Linde, meanwhile, has run the whole gamut from independent, mature and altruistic woman – Nora's contrast – to shipwrecked, envious and destructive spinster, a Gregers Werle in a skirt.

The Helmer children, finally, have been omitted in many productions. As we have seen, the sequences in which they appear help to characterise Nora as a mother. In the 1974 Oslo production, for example, Nora revealed herself to be less of a mother than a 'somewhat hysterical actress enjoying herself by arranging a prank'.[73]

Proxemics – the grouping of the characters with regard to one another and to the audience – is an essential part of every stage production. Where should Nora be placed when she says 'Never see him [Helmer] again', indicating that suicide is on her mind? Demonstratively, by the door in the hall, her hand on the handle, ready to leave? Pathetically, outside the door leading to Helmer's room? By the stove, seeking warmth from it? In the 1981 production at the University of Calgary the director had her say the line looking out of the window.[74] The example illustrates how different proxemic solutions add different connotations to enunciations.

In the otherwise realistic 1972 Stockholm performance, the characters turned to the audience whenever they had something important to say, an alienation effect that was not always appreciated.[75] A similar position was taken by Nora at the end of the 1974 Oslo version. Having taken her decision, she hardly listened to Helmer, faced the audience frontally and looked ahead of it into the unknown future. In the same production, one critic complained, the characters were sometimes placed so far from one another that no intimacy was possible.[76]

With regard to kinesics, William Archer dismissed as 'mere pedantry' Eleonora Duse's refusal (London 1893) 'to give the slightest start' when Krogstad exposed her forgery.[77] And the *New York Times* made the following remark concerning the gestures of Kommisarjevskaya's Nora (New York 1908):

> Some of her stage business such as placing her finger to her lips
> and passing her hand slowly across her forehead were intended to
> indicate mental complexities, but they were perceived as unnecessary
> and distracting mannerisms.[78]

When Alla Nazimova performed the part in the same place and year she seems to have paid particular attention to the paralinguistic aspects. She played the role 'with a passionate intensity that made Nora's transformation at the end completely an inner reality, conveyed in low-pitched, emotion-laden words'.[79] Liv Ullmann has interestingly indicated how even a seemingly banal phrase can be given depth when enunciated in a meaningful way:

> About ten times Nora exclaims: 'Oh, I am so happy!' I choose to
> have her say it without joy – and the last time with sorrow, anxiety
> and longing. . . . Do we need to go around repeating constantly that
> we are happy if we really are?[80]

J. L. Styan reminds us how a combination of kinesics and paralinguistics may clarify the nature of Nora's generosity in sequence 5: 'Performance makes the point: does she give the man [the Porter] the larger coin with a careless air, thus declaring her indifference to money, or does she hesitate for just a moment before she says, "keep the change"?'[81]

As for the linguistic aspect, Hans Heiberg in his review of the 1936 Oslo performance criticised the theatre for lacking respect for

Ibsen. What he meant was not that the text had been too much but too little modernised. 'It is about time the National Theatre understands that Ibsen is too good to be taken literally.'[82] In his New York adaptation a year later Thornton Wilder not only updated the text but also

> americanized the dialogue and eliminated all of Torvald's pet names for Nora such as 'my little squirrel' and 'little skylark'. The removal of these fatuous endearments not only disposed of the saccharine relationship between Torvald and Nora, but also changed their characters.[83]

The tarantella is the climactic scene in most productions of *A Doll's House*. In the 1879 Copenhagen production, according to Edvard Brandes, Mrs Hennings' tarantella lacked that 'sensual abandon' which it requires as 'the erotic high-point of the marriage'.[84] By contrast, Gran found that she danced 'with rhythmic perfection, giving through her body a marvellous expression of the highly complicated feelings' at this point.[85]

As performed by Eleonora Duse (Milan 1891), the tarantella 'was reduced to a quiet sequence in which she donned a crown of roses, seized the tambourine, danced a few tentative steps, and then sank down exhausted in a chair'.[86] While Minnie Maddern Fiske (New York 1894) played down the emotional fervour of the tarantella,[87] the dance was the high point of Ethel Barrymore's 1905 New York performance:

> Barrymore . . . stressed the emotionally harrowing nature of this moment for Nora and conveyed the impression of a girl who held her life in her hands. She danced wildly, frantically.[88]

Vera Kommisarjevskaya's tarantella (New York 1908) 'was no more than a series of expressive poses during which the feet simply tapped out a nervous rhythm. If you watched only the feet it looked more like running than dancing'.[89] Opposed to naturalistic mimetic theatre, Kommisarjevskaya performed the tarantella in a suggestive way, leaving much to the spectator's imagination.

The way Tore Segelcke danced the tarantella (Oslo 1936), 'with the outburst of a temperament rendered unbalanced and rebellious by her sense of loneliness in an erotic game which she, deep down, always experienced as degrading' was in keeping with her playing of the part as a whole. 'From the first moment there was something strained and hysterical about her liveliness.'[90]

In the 1978 Stockholm adaptation, Lena Granhagen's Nora was singing as she performed 'Anitra's dance' from *Peer Gynt* – a combination of the first draft and the published version – in an obviously rehearsed, habitual pattern, a dance without emotions, of someone offering herself. As in the draft version, here it was Mrs Linde rather than the men who accompanied Nora on the piano. 'Mrs Linde takes part in Nora's revolt. Her wild piano playing can hardly be stopped. She too knows what it means to sell yourself in marriage.'[91]

A trend in modern performances is to make the relationship between Nora and Helmer so warm and intimate that the break at the end is like 'a cut into living flesh'.[92] But sometimes, as in the case of Niemann-Raabe, there has been no divorce at the end. In the adapted 1882 Milwaukee ending, Minerva Guernsey's Eve (Nora) was allowed to remain with her family. So was Helena Modjeska's Nora in the 1883 Louisville production:

> She knew that Ibsen had softened the ending for German audiences, so she decided to do the same in America. After some 'indefinite talk about religion', there was a reunion, a rushing together, and a falling curtain on a happy family tableau.[93]

As late as 1955 Ibsen's alternative ending – where Nora remains – was used in a Swedish production.

By contrast, Gabrielle Réjane (Paris 1894) 'left unbroken and as the greater of the two. In this leave-taking scene, she went as some-

5 The cigar scene: Lena Granhagen as Nora and Christer Banck as Doctor Rank in Jan Håkanson's 1978 production at the Stockholm City Theatre.

one who has finally thrown off her own shackles and freed herself.'[94] And Tore Segelcke (Oslo 1936), similarly, left 'erect and calm', indicating to the spectator that her exit was a departure 'into life'.[95]

Bibi Andersson (Stockholm 1972), on the other hand, as a critic remarked, 'does not grow in the final scene: she seems small, frozen and lonely as she exits through the hall door. How will she be able to manage on her own?'[96]

A puzzling ending was provided in the 1985 Gothenburg version, in which the comic aspects of the play were stressed. Nora left – only to return almost immediately. Had she changed her mind? This idea, which must have been in the minds of the audience, was quickly put to shame when it appeared that she had returned merely because, having just given away her keys, she had found the street door locked on the inside for the night. Helmer consequently had to go down and unlock it. Did this unconventional ending indicate that Nora was again being humiliated as she had always been? Or did it, on the contrary, indicate that Helmer was now accepting the fact that his wife was leaving him? Whichever way, this version of the ending was utterly confusing to the audience. It just did not work.

Liv Ullmann has commented interestingly on the way she recreated the leave-taking, and the ideas behind it:

> I believe that Nora's most beautiful declaration and act of love is leaving her husband.
>
> She says goodbye to everything that is familiar and secure. She does not walk through the door to find somebody else to live with and for; she is leaving the house more insecure than she ever realized she could be. But she hopes to find out who she is and why she is.
>
> In this there is a great freedom: the knowledge that I have to part with my present life. I don't know for what. For myself. To be something more than I am now. . . .
>
> It is a little girl who slams the door behind her. A little girl in the process of growing up.[97]

This may be compared to Hans-Christer Sjöberg's description of the 1974 Oslo ending:

> Then the mask is gradually dropped. Her artificial manners disappear one by one. The arms fall down, the voice becomes toneless, the eyes gaze longingly into an unknown future, where maybe the miraculous is to be found. An immense stillness reigns around this scene, where Liv Ullmann is sitting alone in the middle of the room like a clown, who has finished his performance and is resting after it.
>
> Then she gets up, walks slowly upstage and closes the door behind her. She is still the same uncertain woman as in the beginning of the play, but she now at last sees her situation clearly.[98]

Unlike most actresses who have acted Nora in their own language, even when touring abroad, Liv Ullmann encountered the problem of 'changing' from a Norwegian-speaking Nora in Oslo to an English-speaking Nora in New York – a metamorphosis almost as hard as the one Ibsen's heroine undergoes. In Ullmann's words:

> Performing *A Doll's House* in a foreign language after having played it in Norwegian is extremely difficult for me. I set my alarm for 5 a.m. Read and read. Make a lot of changes in the translation because Nora's words are so full of meaning for me. I know them so well, and I think the English translation has missed a lot of what is Nora's distinctive quality.
>
> One of the problems I have is 'washing' the Norwegian text from my head. It is essential for me now to think in English, and if I cannot leave the Norwegian associations behind me, I will never be able to manage this.
>
> Here, I have to acquire a new set of images, a new grid of references. Nora in New York can never be the same as Nora in Oslo.[99]

Just as directors may influence each other, so may actors. Koht assumes that Johanne Dybwad's interpretation 'may have been influenced by Johanne Juell, her mother; she in turn passed the tradition on to Tore Segelcke'.[100] For her role of Nora in the 1925 Stockholm performance Harriet Bosse, according to one critic, had studied Johanne Dybwad's creation of the part. 'But there are things', he added, 'which cannot be imitated, among them spontaneity. Mrs Bosse's naivety was artificial, her voice hard and her glances sometimes far from benevolent.'[101] It is hardly a coincidence that all three actresses shared the same nationality. Since theatre is a language-bound medium, acting traditions tend to correlate with language areas and national heritage.

Another reason why actors and actresses recreate the same role in different ways is that they come to it with different theatrical backgrounds. Earlier roles, especially recent ones, would colour newly adopted ones. In Janet Achurch's later *Doll's House* performances 'the marital clash of Nora and Torvald acquired . . . something of the same passionate anger and bitterness' the actress had earlier brought to the tortured relationship of Rita and Alfred Allmers in Ibsen's *Little Eyolf*.[102] Similarly, 'fresh from one of her greatest successes as Madame Sans-Gêne, Réjane transferred, as it were, the robust spirit of Sardou's pert, saucy washerwoman to Ibsen's heroine [Nora] – a spirit of personal rebelliousness . . .'.[103] By the same token, Liv Ullmann has revealed how her stage incarnation of an unusually independent woman coloured her recreation of Ibsen's heroine:

> I am on the stage, I am Nora, and suddenly discover that she has borrowed life from [Strindberg's] Queen Christina, whom I have previously portrayed. Nora has movements she did not have the first time I played the part, nuances in the voice I had not previously associated with her – but which emerged from the interaction between me and the Swedish queen.[104]

After this survey of how the play has been handled on the stage, let us look a little more closely at three individual productions, those of Hans Neuenfels and Ingmar Bergman.

In his 1972 Stuttgart production, transferred to Frankfurt the year after, Neuenfels approached the play in a startlingly new way. Clearly post-absurdist, his *Nora* revealed the Helmer marriage, synecdochic of the society sanctioning it, as a relationship built on empty forms, role-playing and lack of communication. All the characters were puppets pulled by unseen strings. Even tender moments between them seemed artificial. The characters switched abruptly from one mood to another and turned dialogue into monologues, as they looked towards the audience instead of at one another. Some time before she made her final exit, Nora rehearsed her leave-taking before the mirror. In this way Neuenfels indicated how the characters were narcissistically unable to communicate with each other.

The setting, designed by Klaus Gelhaar, showed a very large room, stiffly symmetrical: a huge window in the rear; on either side of it a huge door and a mirror upstage and a high urn downstage; in the centre a tripartite sofa, indicating that isolationism prevailed even in this pronouncedly 'communicative' piece of furniture. Above the doors were large emblematic figures, symbolising Nora's divided self and transformation from kitten (left) to lioness (right). In the first two acts she concomitantly had dark, well-groomed hair; after her change of costume in Act III this was replaced by a reddish mane.

Rather than an attractive, realistic living-room, Neuenfels' setting seemed to display the Room of Life as the Waiting-Room of Death.[105] The gigantic proportions of the room made the people in it seem small. The poisonously cool green of the interior – the green of this earth? – as opposed to the attractive blue sky seen beyond the enormous window helped to accentuate the metaphysical connotations of the production, where Nora's exit was not downwards through the street-door but upwards through the window. The setting seemed to have almost as much in common with Strindberg's theatre corridor, in *A Dream Play*, as with Ibsen's living-room.

Like the setting, the lighting was unrealistic. When Marianne – Ibsen's Anne-Marie – closed the curtains in the final act, it was black outside the window, as we would expect. Yet when Nora shortly afterwards parted the curtains, the sky was blue. Rather than assume that Neuenfels, unlike Ibsen, had his version end in daytime, black and blue here stood for Nora's contrasting feelings: suicidal thoughts versus a sense of liberation. That blue signified hope and freedom was indicated also by the fact that the paper bag, containing the 'revolutionary' macaroons, with which Nora waved Helmer farewell, was sky-coloured, light blue.

Nora was dressed in a white blouse and a long brown skirt throughout most of the play. Rather than a Neapolitan folk costume, she wore a white dress for the tarantella. Mrs Linde, in her lilac silk costume, looked as though she too was going to attend the Stenborg fancy dress ball. Both women were set off against the men, all of them in different shades of grey or black.

A remarkable directorial device was the handling of the Nurse, dressed in masculine grey. Constantly hovering around her mistress, Marianne was turned into the animus or superego within Nora.[106] At one point she kept prompting Nora, repeating the word 'Verplichtungen' (duties), as Nora read from a prompter's script. Especially in this sequence, it was obvious that Nora and Marianne represented one and the same figure.

The curtain rose on a *tableau vivant*, emblematising the social and conjugal man–woman relations. Nora was seen reclining on the sofa, while above her, in the large window, the black silhouette of an erect Helmer with bowler hat – the attribute of a banker – could be perceived. The suppressed woman at home was pitted against the suppressing man outside, in society. At the end of the play, this situation was reversed. Helmer was now sitting in the middle of the sofa, his arms outstretched like those of a crucified, while Nora, having left her doll's house, was standing above him in the window, indicating that she would return and take over the regime – an ending indicative of the militant attitude of the women's liberation movement in the early 1970s.

The performance was full of explicit visual metaphors, in the surrealist or absurdist tradition. Neuenfels had Helmer find Nora's hidden macaroon bag; whereupon he took her by the ear, as a father might his mischievous daughter. Nora, full of hysterical energy, tried to compensate for her unsatisfied love by embracing not only people but also objects around her. The children entered holding on to a thick rope, placed themselves on the sofa, silently staring in front of them, while Nora, she too staring before her, was talking to them – an emblematic tableau of paternal drill and maternal chill.

Although Neuenfels was adhering rather faithfully to Ibsen's dialogue, he combined it with kinesics that completely altered the meaning of the words. Whereas Rank's 'Thanks for the light' in the text on a superficial level refers to the fact that Nora has just lit his cigar, the phrase became absurd with Neuenfels since his Rank never let his cigar be lit by Nora but, on the contrary, crumbled it. In the play text, similarly, Krogstad's 'You don't do such things' refers to

6 Nora's (Elisabeth Trissenaar) spectacular exit above Helmer
(Peter Roggisch) through the window in Hans Neuenfels' 1972
production at the Stuttgart–Württemberg State Theatre.

Nora's indication that she might commit suicide. But since Neuenfels had Nora throw her hat through the window at this moment, Krogstad's remark seemed to be a reaction not so much to her words as to her bizarre action.

During the tarantella which was played not on a 'live' instrument (piano) but on a mechanical one (gramophone), Nora stood completely still. When the music stopped she fell to the floor. Since the tarantella was repeated in Act III, now with the drunken Rank as a dancer, the impression that this was indeed a dance for the dying, a dance of death, was strongly conveyed.

Although Neuenfels' unconventional *Doll's House* version is a fairly extreme case, the director's approach is rather symptomatic of the manner in which Ibsen is nowadays staged in Germany. While Scandinavian and British Ibsen productions still tend to be safely anchored in the realistic tradition, German ones demonstrate a greater desire to break loose from this tradition. Ingmar Bergman, who is thoroughly acquainted both with the Swedish and the German theatre, may be seen as a fruitful synthesis of these diverging endeavours.

Bergman's two *Doll's House* productions, presented in different countries with a time lapse of some eight years, interestingly demonstrate how two versions of the same play by the same director compare.

On 30 April 1981 Bergman's *Nora*, as the play is often called in Germany, opened at the Residenztheater in Munich.[107] Virtually the same text formed the basis for his second production of the play, opening on 17 November 1989 at the Swedish equivalent of the Residenztheater, the Royal Dramatic Theatre in Stockholm. The play now carried the traditional Swedish title *Ett dockhem*.

We can only expect a performance intended for a south German audience in the early 1980s to be different in some respects from one intended for a Swedish one around 1990. Besides the temporal differences, there was the spatial one between one country and another, the sociopolitical climate in Franz Josef Strauss' Bavaria being rather different from that in Sweden. There was the linguistic difference, a German translation of Ibsen's play being necessarily more removed from the Dano-Norwegian source text than a Swedish one. Moreover, in Munich Bergman was forced to deal with a language which was not his own. In Stockholm, by contrast, he was in that respect on a par with his actors, whose social and cultural referential system agreed more or less with his own. The different theatrical traditions in the two countries were another point of importance. The characteristics of the individual actors, finally, necessarily made one Nora differ from another, one Helmer from another.

In addition to these general differences, a more specific one may be added. In Munich *Nora* was part of a kind of trilogy, the other plays being Strindberg's *Miss Julie*, here called simply *Julie*, and Bergman's own *Scenes from a Marriage*, a rather radical stage adaptation of the famous television series. As the titles indicate, the link between the three plays was the focusing upon man–woman relations: Helmer–Nora, Jean–Julie, Johan–Marianne. The plays were produced simultaneously and the 'trilogy' soon came to be known as 'the Bergman project'. In Stockholm, by contrast, *A Doll's House* was presented as an independent play.

The focusing upon the Helmer–Nora relationship at the Residenztheater – the characters were played by Robert Atzorn and Rita Russek – meant that the three Helmer children prescribed by Ibsen as well as their Nurse were visually eliminated. The ruling idea behind the production was Nora's emancipatory conviction that she has a right – nay, an obligation – to leave her husband and the consequences this has for him and him alone.

Ibsen's play was drastically cut; nearly one third of the text was removed. The three acts of the original were replaced by fifteen scenes (in Stockholm increased to sixteen). And the unity of setting gave way to the presentation of three different rooms of the Helmer apartment: the living-room, the dining-room, the bedroom. Even so, Bergman retained a strong sense of claustrophobia, since both windows and doors were lacking in the tall wainscoting surrounding the room; not until the end, when Nora made her exit, was a closet door in the background surprisingly revealed. Nora finally found a way out of her sombre 'prison'. This device was in a sense a quotation from Strindberg's *The Father*, as performed at the Stockholm City Theatre, where Gunilla Palmstierna-Weiss had been responsible for another seemingly doorless, imprisoning living-room. This performance preceded the production of *Nora* by less than two months.

A sense of claustrophobia was also ensured by the fact that the whole play was acted out on an inner stage, a quadrilateral platform, surrounded by extremely high walls topped by small barred windows. The intention behind the setting was not so much to suggest that the Helmer marriage is imprisoning, even less to visualise a fear on Nora's part that she may be imprisoned once her forgery has been discovered. Since the representative quality of the Helmer–Nora relationship was stressed throughout, and since the high dark-red, velvet walls at the back of the stage were suspiciously theatrical, the audience was invited to mirror itself in what was happening on the stage.

A striking aspect of the performance – repeated in many other Bergman productions – was the fact that the actors never disappeared out of sight. Exits were indicated simply by their leaving the platform stage for the background, where they remained sitting until their next 'entrance'. With this device Bergman placed his production in an illusion-breaking Pirandellian and Brechtian tradition, indicating the constant flux between onstage and offstage role-playing, between theatre and life. By letting the actors, when off-platform, form a stage audience, Bergman provided a link between them and the real audience. Combined with the barred windows of the setting, the impression of the stage audience was one of a jury in a court-room sitting in judgement on the marital relationship that was acted out before their eyes and in which they themselves, when onstage, were directly or indirectly involved. The stage audience could in this way mediate between the acting onstage characters and the observing real audience. By this arrangement the idea was strengthened that the spectators in the auditorium, as mentally divided as the characters-cum-actors, were virtually sitting in judgement upon themselves.

As in the source text, the action in *Nora* was set around 1880. On the curtain the scene designer had drawn a street in Christiania, showing the exterior of the Helmer apartment house. When the curtain parted, the audience moved, as it were, from the exterior to the interior of the Helmer apartment. This 'zoom-in' may have been inspired by the progression in Strindberg's *Ghost Sonata*, a play which Bergman has produced three times. The characters wore the stiff clothes of the 1880s, high collars and grey or black dresses for the grey-haired men, a corseted wine-red dress for Nora – a vivid spot in a grey world.

The play opened, not with Nora's entering the apartment together with the Porter, as Ibsen has it, but with Nora

> already seated, utterly immobile, in the midst of a wilderness of toys,
> dolls, and other suggestive relics of childhood. Leaning back against
> the pillows of the [wine-red] plush sofa, she stared out into empty
> space – virtually the picture of a human doll waiting to be taken
> up and played with. The very distant and faintly audible sound of
> an old-fashioned music-box tune [Schumann's *Träumerei* from
> *Kinderszenen*] added to the strongly oneiric mood of nostalgia
> and suppressed melancholy that was created by this silent image
> of her motionless, oddly dejected figure.[108]

With her wine-red dress Nora was at one with the comfortable sofa she was reclining in – a visual metaphor of the confining unity between character and environment. Among the 'relics of childhood' was a doll's bed, ironically foreshadowing the marital double bed shown at the end.[109] Nora's claim that she has been treated as a doll first by her father, then by her husband seemed visually corroborated by this correspondence.

Unlike his *Nora*, Bergman's *Doll's House* was set around the turn of the century. The union flags in the Christmas tree indicated that the action took place not later than 1905, when the union between Sweden and Norway was dissolved. By this change the distance between the original sender (Ibsen) and the receiver (the Stockholm audience) was diminished by some twenty-five years. Moving the play closer to our time not only increased the audience's sense of being in touch with the characters. Nora's emancipatory ideas and her willingness to break out of her marriage also seemed more plausible. The fashion around 1905 helped to make the bodies, especially Nora's, physically – erotically – present. Last but not least, since the opening took place in one of the most beautiful *art nouveau* buildings in Stockholm – the Royal Dramatic Theatre was completed in 1908 – the period selected was a kind of homage to the theatre which Bergman has come to see as his professional home. The blue *Jugendstil* curtain of the Royal Dramatic Theatre for once functioned not as a border separating the stage from the auditorium. Rather, it suggested the temporal unity between these two areas.

As in Munich, the play was acted out on a quadrilateral platform surrounded by walls eleven metres high, topped by eight small barred windows. 'The little room – the home – is placed inside a larger room which is society', Leif Zern wrote, and this larger room 'in the course of the evening is transformed into a universe, a human cosmos, a home on earth'.[110] By surrounding the Helmer home with a large dark space, Bergman diminished the characters, turned them into dolls, and set their little world off from the big, threatening one outside. As in Munich, the actors remained visible also when they were offstage. However, they were this time not seated in the background but on either side, immediately below the raised inner stage.

On this stage, representing the living-room, a green *art nouveau* sofa and armchair could be seen, as well as a decorated Christmas tree and a heap of parcels. Behind the platform a green-tinted bourgeois *art nouveau* dining-room could be divined: round table, chairs, piano, and above the centrally placed piano a large painting.[111] Reminiscent of a picture out of a photo album, the setting seemed to indicate Nora's dual vacillation between the world of the present and of reality (foreground) and the world of the past and of fantasy (background), the green colour bridging the two worlds. The green could be associated both with hope as in Strindberg's *Dream Play*, several times staged by Bergman, or with an imprisoning aquarium existence, as in his 1988 production of O'Neill's *Long Day's Journey into Night.*

In the second scene the foreground shifted from green living-room to brown dining-room, while the background, still green-tinted, now displayed a sideboard with two candelabras, above it a flowery *art nouveau* wallpaper and, as in the former scene, a large painting. The brown colour, characteristic of the *Jugendstil* but here associated rather with bourgeois materialism, was now set off against the green of the background. With Krogstad's appearance, the distance between imprisoning, earthy reality and lofty dream – the candelabras turned the background sideboard into a kind of altar – had increased. The round table on the platform was mirrored in an almost identical one in the background 'photo', creating an eerie, dreamlike effect. The impression that the play was acted out in two different worlds – a three-dimensional, real one and a two-dimensional, imaginary one – was hereby strengthened. Since the projected furniture in the background appeared larger than the real one in the foreground, the doll's house connotations of the scenery were further underscored.

An aged Rank appeared in an elegant *fin-de-siècle* costume, whereas a young successful Torvald Helmer was fashioned according to the *dernier cri* in *art nouveau.* Krogstad could be seen in a coat green of mould, while Mrs Linde was dressed completely in black as though she was in mourning – although her husband had been dead for three years. Her costume was clearly designed to correspond to that of Nora at the end of the play, where it became clear that Nora had taken over Mrs Linde's outgrown role. Nora first appeared in a pink dress with a green apron, on which a small N was inscribed inside a big H – one of those meaningful details characteristic of a Bergman stage production. Later she appeared in her black-and-white Capri costume, underneath which a bright red petticoat could be divined. She also wore a black shawl – as prescribed by Ibsen. When Helmer had read the first, threatening letter from Krogstad, he angrily ordered her to take off her shawl. It was an act of unmasking. When he had read the second, conciliatory letter, he protectively laid the shawl around her shoulders. The mask was put back in place.

Ibsen's Nora leaves not only her husband but also her three small children. Today, when most people would accept that a wife might divorce her husband if she finds their marriage hollow and meaningless, many would still claim that the presence of young children should prevent her from doing so.

The visual absence of the children in *Nora*, Bergman eventually discovered, was a mistake. Yet in a simplified staging, three children plus a nurse, the director and his stage designer realised, is a nuisance. Besides, leaving three – or even two – children 'motherless' is less sad than leaving just one child behind. After all, two or three children have one another. Consequently, in *A Doll's House* Bergman settled for one child, a daughter, Hilde, who looked about six or seven. Appearing only at the beginning and end of the play, Hilde was nevertheless symbolically present throughout the performance in the form of her doll, seated on one of the chairs next to the acting area.

When the play opened, Nora was sitting on the sofa reading the end of a fairy tale to her almost identically dressed daughter: '. . . but a prince and his bride brought with them as much silver as they could carry. And they moved to the castle east of the sun and west of the moon.' The reading was accompanied by sweet, romantic piano music, 'The Maiden's Prayer', as from a music-box. Having received a goodnight kiss from her mother, Hilde left for bed. Nora lay down on the sofa, whistling the tune that had just been heard, put one arm in the air, then let it fall to the floor as her whistling petered out.

What Bergman presented in this opening was an emblematic situation, a key to Nora's existence: her desire to see life in terms of a fairy tale (with its obligatory happy ending) and her vague awareness that life is anything but that. Very effectively Bergman demonstrated how Nora, who as a single child had herself – figuratively speaking – been brought up on fairy tales by her father, now continued this tradition with regard to *her* single daughter. Three generations were implicitly interwoven in this initial *tableau vivant*, suggesting a. *perpetuum mobile.*

Sitting on the floor, Nora then began to unwrap the Christmas presents, while calling for her husband: 'Come out, Torvald, and see what I've bought.' From a realistic point of view this might seem strange, but what was important here was that the audience should see that Nora had bought her daughter a doll for a Christmas present. The deeper significance of this was not revealed until the end of the performance.

When Helmer joined Nora behind the Christmas parcels, they looked like two little children – in accordance with the Bergmanian idea that grown-ups are merely children masquerading as grown-ups. As we have seen, psychological role-playing was continually stressed in the production.

'As far as I understand', Strindberg writes in his preface to *Getting Married*, 'Nora offers herself for sale – to be paid for in cash.'[112] Strindberg's idea that Nora 'prostitutes' herself was utilised already in the opening of the performance. After all, Bergman seemed to argue, it is not the Nora–Rank relationship that is corrupt but the Nora–Helmer one. This was demonstrated in the initial monetary scene, which was done as follows:

HELMER *still sitting on the floor frontstage, takes out his wallet.* Nora, what do you suppose I have here?

NORA *who has been standing by the Christmas tree in the background, jumps onto the sofa, triumphantly shouting.* Money!

HELMER Good heavens, of course I realise it costs a lot to run a house at Christmas time.

NORA *still on the sofa, picks one banknote after another out of* HELMER's *open wallet – after each approving nod by him.* Ten, twenty, thirty – *He closes the wallet but opens it again and lets her have one more.* Forty. Oh thank you, Torvald, thank you. I'll make this go a long way.

HELMER And what have you thought of for yourself?

NORA What, for me? I don't want anything.

HELMER Of course you do. Name something that you'd like to have –
within reason, of course.

NORA No, I really don't know. As a matter of fact, though, Torvald …

HELMER Well?

NORA *embraces him.* If you really want to give me something, you
could of course – you could –

HELMER *embraces her.* Come on, let's have it!

NORA *lies back on the floor and drags him with her.* You could give me
money, Torvald. *Stretching her legs in the air on either side of* HELMER,
who is lying on top of her. Only as much as you think you can spare. Then
I could buy something for it. (*seq. 7*)

Here the nature of Helmer's and Nora's marriage is emblematically
depicted. The coitus position demonstrates how *she* is offering her
body in exchange for the money *he* has just been offering her. Their
marriage – representative as it is – is no more than legalised prostitution. By presenting the Helmer marriage as starkly as this, Bergman
provided a logical basis for Nora's decision at the end to free herself
from a relationship which was degrading for both of them. The passage seemed choreographically designed to contrast with Nora's attitude at the end, where she refuses to accept anything from her husband.

Strindberg's severe criticism of Nora refers not to the monetary
scene but to her exhibiting her silk-stockings to Rank. In Bergman's
interpretation, this passage suggested anything but 'prostitution' on
Nora's part:

NORA *is standing behind* RANK, *who is sitting on a chair. Both face the
audience. She puts her hands on his shoulders.*

NORA Be nice now. *Puts her hands over his eyes.* Tomorrow you'll see how
well I'll dance. And that I do it only for you. And for Torvald, of course.
Removes her hands.

NORA I'll show you something. *Takes up one of her black silk-stockings, shakes it, has it glide down across his forehead to his eyes.*

NORA Silk-stockings. *Removes the stocking from his eyes, lifts it up.* Aren't they beautiful? It's very dark in here now, of course, but tomorrow –. But how critical you look! Don't you think they'll fit me? *Puts the stocking around* RANK's *neck.*

RANK I can't really give you a qualified opinion on that. NORA *looks at him, smilingly.* Shame on you!   (*seq.39*)

Substituting black stockings for Ibsen's 'flesh-coloured' ones and omitting Nora's 'Oh well, I suppose you can look a bit higher if you want to', Bergman was clearly not interested in emphasising the erotic relationship between Nora and Rank. Rather, the scene stressed the fact that they have the idea of imminent death in common. When Nora covered Rank's eyes with her black stocking, she visually turned him into a victim before an executioner. When she put the stocking around his neck, she provided another 'death sentence'. Yet since the stocking belonged to Nora, who is herself a victim of circumstances and who may well be contemplating suicide already at this point – in sequence 46 this is manifestly so – both gestures applied also to her. The subtext of Bergman's version was not 'What a pity we can't sleep together.' It was rather a consoling – and self-consoling – ritual, worthy of a Hedda Gabler, suggesting that death is 'beautiful'.

The ending was set in the Helmer bedroom.[113] In the background the living-room and the dining-room could, again, be seen as huge 'photographs'. As Nora contemplated her past life with Helmer, the three rooms visualised, as it were, their eight years together. The photo connotation seemed especially relevant when Nora was about to take leave of this existence and transform it into a remembrance of things past. At the end, Tove Ellefsen wrote, Bergman's *Doll's House* 'turns into scenes from a marriage, into distant pictures of an old photo album, where soft shades finally change into modern black-and-white'.[114]

The idea behind the change of setting – in both productions –

7   The stocking scene as presented by Ingmar Bergman in his 1989
production at the Royal Dramatic Theatre in Stockholm. Nora (Pernilla
Östergren) is seen standing behind Doctor Rank (Erland Josephson).

was that husband and wife have gone to bed together. He believes that she has reconciled herself with him. She is inclined to think that this is their last night together. When the sequence opened, revealing a slender white *art nouveau* double bed with a glaring red bedspread, Helmer was seen asleep in it. As Nora entered, dressed in a simple black, timeless coat and carrying a small travelling-bag, he woke up. In the dark part of the stage on the left Nora was now standing, fully dressed in 'mourning'. To the right, bathed in a searing white light, Helmer was sitting in bed stark naked – defenceless, unmasked. On the bedpost hung the red jester's cap he had worn at the fancy-dress ball the night before. While explaining her new position to him, Nora moved back and forth from the shade on the left to the brightly lit area on the right, from isolation to communion – as though she was struggling with the question: to leave or not to leave. The ending was enacted as follows:

HELMER *sitting to the right in the double bed, looking down.* Nora, – can I never be anything but a stranger to you?

NORA *standing on the left, the travelling-bag in her hand.* Oh, Torvald, then the most wonderful thing would have to happen –

HELMER *looks up.* Name it, this most wonderful thing!

NORA *puts the bag down, walks up to the bed.* You and I would both have to change so much that – Oh, Torvald . . . I don't believe in wonders any more. *She turns and goes left, half covering her face with one hand. Takes the black shawl in her left hand, the bag in her right one.*

HELMER But I'll believe in them. Tell me! Change so much that – ?

NORA *turns away from him, wipes her eyes with her handkerchief, picks up her travelling-bag, turns around and looks at him, in a warm but firm voice.* That our marriage became a life together. *Pause. Turns away.* Goodbye. *Exits left.*

HELMER Nora. Nora! Nora!! *The front door slams shut. Whispers.* Nora. *Darkness, curtain.* (*seq. 76–7*)

Bergman's skilful choreography could be sensed in this unconventional way of ending the play. While most directors would have

8 Nora's leave-taking of Helmer (Per Mattsson) as visualised by Ingmar Bergman in his 1989 production at the Royal Dramatic Theatre in Stockholm. Between them, in the background, their daughter Hilde. To the left, off-platform, Mrs Linde (Marie Richardson) and Krogstad (Björn Granath).

Nora answer Helmer's question concerning 'the most wonderful thing' straight away, Bergman inserted a pause at this point to ensure maximum suspense. In this way, the audience was given time to wonder, with Helmer, what the most wonderful thing might be – and so to feel empathy with him. In addition, the pause gave proper weight to Nora's key sentence.

In the source text, we recall, this line reads: 'At samliv mellem os to kunde bli'e et ægteskab' (That our life together could become a marriage.) For Ibsen 'marriage' was the loaded word. For Bergman, offering his version to a present-day audience, it was rather 'life together' that seemed a viable concept. The director cleverly updated the play – thereby adjusting it to the changes in man–woman relations during the last hundred years – simply by having the two key words change places: 'Att vårt äktenskap blev ett samliv.'

Shortly before Nora left, Hilde appeared on the stage, silently watching her mother's leave-taking. Woken up by the shouting of the parents, she now became a witness to what was nothing like the fairy-tale ending Nora had provided her with before she went to bed. Hilde now wore a blue dress, similar in style to the one Nora had been wearing in the beginning, and carried the (similarly dressed) doll she had just received from her mother. The device came close to what the Dutch refer to as 'Droste effect', so called after the chocolate packets showing a nurse carrying a Droste packet on her tray, this packet again showing a nurse carrying a Droste packet on her tray, this packet . . . – *ad infinitum*. Left alone with her father – just as Nora had once been left alone with *her* father – Hilde seemed doomed to relive Nora's experience. Deprived of her mother and lacking a sister or brother, Hilde would have to console herself by playing the role of mother to her doll. In his ending Bergman clearly outlined the vicious circle in which the child with just one parent finds itself – a central issue in a social environment where divorces tend to be the rule rather than the exception.

When Nora made her final exit from the platform stage, she passed by Mrs Linde and Krogstad sitting next to it. The happily united couple was proxemically – and ironically – contrasted with the separating marital partners. While the Munich Nora, as we have noted, left through a closet door at the back of the stage, the Stockholm Nora left via the auditorium – as if she were a member of the audience, departing from the theatre along with them. This was an ending very much in the spirit suggested in Chevrel's study of the play, published the same year:

> Un metteur en scène a-t-il imaginé de faire jouer *Maison de poupée* en costumes contemporains de sa mise en scène et, à la fin, pendant qu'Helmer reste seul en scène, de faire venir Nora dans la salle, de lui faire prendre place parmi les spectateurs?
>
> Mais le rideau, alors, pourrait-il se baisser?[115]

Characteristic of both the Munich and the Stockholm production was the reliance on a heavily adapted version, in which much of Ibsen's concern for realistic plausibility – what we now see as surface realism – was done away with. As a result, a stylised psychological drama came to the fore in which the characters via their offstage counterparts were related to the audience. This attempt to bridge the gulf between stage and auditorium was especially noticeable in the Stockholm version, where the drama was acted out on a 'timeless', 'universal' platform between the *art nouveau* decor in the background and the *art nouveau* auditorium in front. An earlier plan to have Nora appear also in *art nouveau* clothes at the end was discarded in favour of a more anonymous, less time-specific costume, which could render her more representative and relate her better to the audience.

While Nora's emancipation was the central issue in the version presented to the relatively unemancipated Bavarian audience, it was rather the consequences of her departure for her single daughter – read: the next generation – that formed the final impression in the version offered to the Swedish audience, an audience increasingly aware of the problems pertaining to the children of parents belonging to the divorcing generation. To put it differently: while the

Munich production focused on the marital relationship, the Stockholm one broadened the perspective. At the end, little Hilde vivified not only the present situation. She also represented Nora as a child – Nora, too, having been suddenly bereaved of a parent. By implication – the doll in her arms – she suggested her own future single-parent role. As in the opening of this production, three generations were in this way combined, suggesting a fateful *perpetuum mobile.*[116]

Despite these differences – relating to differences at the producing and receiving end – both the Munich and the Stockholm versions could be classified as typical Bergman productions in the sense that they signified a skilful orchestration of the many instruments that, properly attuned to one another, result in an outstanding and memorable performance.

An acute sense of rhythm and a careful moment-by-moment distribution of theatrical signifiers are two of the most striking features of Bergman's craftsmanship. As a choreographer of moving stage images – moving in both senses of the word – he holds a unique position in the contemporary directorial landscape. His two productions of *A Doll's House* bear witness to this.

CHAPTER 5

'A DOLL'S HOUSE' AS
RADIO DRAMA

Radio drama based on texts written for the stage can strictly speaking be of two kinds: plays which have been adapted and produced directly for the radio, and stage versions which have been transformed into radio plays. In the latter case the actors must switch from stage to radio acting. The advantage of this indirect way of arriving at a radio performance is that the actors are exceedingly familiar with the play, having first rehearsed it and then played it on the stage. It is doubtful whether this advantage outbalances the disadvantage that they may find it difficult to get rid of acting features that rely on the visual code, a code that is no longer available to them.

Radio drama is an intimate form of drama. Deprived of any visual correlative, the listener, like a blind person, will be very sensitive to aural nuances. The actor close to the microphone may be compared with the actor close to the camera in a television or film production. The listener constantly partakes, so to speak, of aural close-ups. Without access to the visual code, (s)he will often find it difficult to keep track of the various characters and to distinguish their voices from one another. To meet these problems, radio favours plays with few roles.

The scenery that is physically present on the stage must somehow be made mentally present for the listener, so that (s)he becomes familiar with the environment surrounding the characters. This can be done via a narrator or by incorporating the stage-directions in the dialogue. Sound-effects can also help to provide an equivalent of the cinematic establishing-shot.

Characteristic of radio drama is the relatively short playing time, motivated by the fact that it is embedded in and competing with a continuous flow of other programmes. Transforming plays intended for the stage into this mode therefore usually entails a considerable abridging of the text.

Ibsen's *A Doll's House* lends itself to radio production. With its unity of time and place, its few roles, its strong reliance on the spoken word and its limited dependence on visual effects, it is in fact more adaptable to radio than most plays written for the stage. But while the playing time in the theatre would normally be around two and a half hours, a radio version is likely to last an hour less.[1] This poses the basic problem of radio adaptation: what can be most easily dispensed with?

Minor characters may be omitted. While Ibsen provides the Helmer household with both a Maid and a Nurse, radio versions will usually let one character fulfil the tasks of both these servants. In Ernst Eklund's 1947 production, the Nurse is retained, while in Lars-Levi Læstadius' 1953 version, it is the Maid, Helene, who is kept.

The entrances and exits of characters must be clearly identified by means of – often added – brief standard expressions. Even so it may be difficult to grasp exactly when a character is alone. This is why soliloquies are usually enunciated in a whispering voice. In the radio versions just referred to, some of the early soliloquies are omitted or – in the 1953 version – replaced by Nora's gradually less cheerful singing of a children's song.

When the opening passage is omitted in radio presentations, it is simply due to the fact that plot value – relating to the dramatic build up of the play – ranks higher than thematic value, relating to the play texture. And the plot value of the opening sequences is low.

This is how three Swedish radio-script versions, in English rendering, open. The first one, from 1944, directed by Ernst Eklund, reads:

NORA ... Helene!
HELENE Yes.

NORA Pay the porter and hide the Christmas tree. The children mustn't
see it until tonight, when it is decorated. You understand?
HELENE Yes, ma'am! *Out. Door.*

Here the presence of the Porter is announced in Nora's second
speech, while the first sign of Nora's spendthrift mentality has been
left out. In another radio version from 1947, directed by Alf
Sjöberg, the whole opening has been cut; the play starts with Nora's
'Come out here, Torvald, and see what I've bought.' Læstadius'
1953 version, finally, begins in a surprisingly conventional manner:

NARRATOR The action takes place in the home of Torvald Helmer, a
lawyer, in the 1880s.
*Jingle of sleigh-bells at a distance. An old-fashioned doorbell rings. A door is
opened.*
NORA *at a distance.* How do you do, Helene! – Hide the Christmas
tree well. The children mustn't see it until tonight, when it is decorated.
HELENE Yes, ma'am.
NORA *approaches humming.*

In this last instance the listener is in very orderly fashion informed
about time and place both by a narrator and by sound effects (bells).

Despite the music that goes with it, the tarantella is above all a
visual spectacle. In a radio production it is hard to find acoustic
equivalents for Nora's anguished dancing. In Sjöberg's version the
passage is kept short; Nora's anguish is conveyed by hysterical laugh-
ter; Helmer instructs her in a more specified way than in the play
text; and Rank seems to accompany her on the piano throughout. In
Læstadius' version, the music is sombre, the tambourine prominent.
In a Dutch version, from 1987, directed by Bert Dijkstra, Helmer,
at the piano, slows down as he asks Nora to dance less wildly. In
none of these versions is there, surprisingly enough, any marked difference between Helmer's way of playing and Rank's.

'Hearing doors being opened and closed each time a character
enters a room', Esslin points out, 'is tedious and often unnecessary
for the listener, yet at the moment when the wife finally deserts her

husband . . . a slammed door has an immense and immediate dramatic and symbolic impact.'[2] Nora's final door slam naturally has a particular relevance to a medium solely dependent on aural communication. Should it be an objective or a subjective sound? Should it be a recognisable, realistic door slam or a sound representing Helmer's experience of it at this moment? No ordinary sound of a closing door would do, William Ash says, when it concerns a door 'clanging shut on a young man who has been condemned to life imprisonment. . . . What is required is a sound like the slamming shut of the gates of Paradise behind our guilty first parents reverberating on and on down the ages.'[3]

Although the example is applicable to Helmer's situation, none of the Swedish radio directors have opted for a subjective door slam:

> NORA   That our life together could become a marriage. Goodbye, Torvald. *Door.*   (*Eklund*)

> NORA   That our life together could become a marriage. Goodbye, Torvald.   (*Sjöberg*)

> NORA   That our life together could become a marriage. Goodbye. *Door.*
> HELMER   *in tears.* Nora! Nora! Empty. She's gone. The most wonderful–? *Street door.*   (*Læstadius*)

After Nora's strong line, which can be rendered in Swedish without any loss, the three versions all reveal slight variations. The third keeps the laconic 'Goodbye' of the original, while the other two add a friendly 'Torvald'. Helmer's final reaction is retained only in the third version. In the second one even the final door slam has been omitted – as it has in the Norwegian 1971 radio production, where Nora's 'Goodbye' is followed by an indication that she leaves only through the apartment door. The absence of the door slam is certainly surprising in a medium dependent solely on the aural code. Did the directors wish to keep the door open for a possible return on Nora's part? Even more surprising is the closing line of the

Norwegian version:

HELMER Nora. She's gone.
  NORA The wonderful thing.

Here Helmer's final words have been given to Nora. Yet since Nora has already left the apartment, the idea is apparently that what we hear is actually Nora's voice as it keeps reverberating inside Helmer. However, by letting Nora refer to 'the wonderful thing' rather than, as Ibsen has it, 'the most wonderful thing', the director blurs the idea that Nora undergoes a change in the course of the play.[4]

In the Dutch radio version, broadcast in two parts with a week's interval, the end is as follows, in English translation:

NORA Then so much will have to change that our life together will become a true life together. *Door, footsteps, street door, wind.*
HELMER Nora! *Close to microphone.* Nora! – Gone. She's gone. – Life together?
Sombre piano music in crescendo.

Here, presumably in an attempt to update the play, the word 'ægteskab' (marriage) is not, as one would expect, translated with 'huwelijk' but with 'samenleven' (life together), the same word as used to translate 'samliv'. The repetition makes the line seem trite and vacuous. The door slam, here occurring not after Helmer's final speech, as Ibsen has it, but before it, is followed by the sound of the wind – a sign of the hostility of the world outside the doll's house and thus of the life Nora is now confronting, or, alternatively, of the harshness experienced by Helmer, now left alone. Far from indicating a dawning of hope on his part, this version, ending with sombre piano music, stresses Helmer's desperate sense of isolation. Although Ibsen's door slam is here again handled realistically, Dijkstra concludes his adaptation with non-diegetic mood music, that is, on a subjective note.

CHAPTER 6

'A DOLL'S HOUSE' AS TELEPLAY

The fundamental difference between stage and screen drama is that whereas stage drama relies on continuous space, screen drama – in our case adaptations for film and television – depends on discontinuous space. While in stage drama we remain visually in the same environment within each act/scene, in screen drama the visible surroundings will change with each shot. And while in the 'democratic' stage drama we have, in principle at least, the freedom to focus on whatever we like on the stage, in the more 'authoritarian' screen drama the camera will successively turn our attention to whatever the director wishes us to see.

Within the screen media there is the basic distinction between film and television, between the big and the small screen, between high and low density, between a 'hot' medium, containing a high amount of data and a 'cool' one containing a limited amount.[1] In our context this is important, since few dramas are adapted for the big screen, whereas most teleplays are adapted stage dramas.[2] Either medium makes use of close-ups. This is especially true of television, which has been called 'a close-up medium'. And there is, in either medium, the difference between black-and-white and colour productions. Of the seven television productions dealt with in this chapter, Åke Falck's (1958) and Michael Kehlmann's (1961) are in black-and-white, whereas Per Sjöstrand's (1970), Palle Kjærulff-Schmidt's (1974), Arild Brinchmann's (1974), Rainer Werner Fassbinder's (1976) and David Thacker's (1991) are in colour.

Within television we may further distinguish between 'live' studio productions, belonging to the early days of television, taped productions enabling editing, and adaptations of stage productions;

between 'theatrical' productions, showing merely interiors, and 'filmic' ones, where exteriors will intermingle with interiors.[3]

On the transmission side there is, of course, much variety in both media, depending on what kind of equipment the recipient is confronted with: width of film strip, size of screen, mono- or stereo-sound, and so on.

A quite different distinction concerns the attitude to the play text, in this case *A Doll's House*. Whereas Falck, Kehlmann, Brinchmann and Thacker adhere rather faithfully to it, Sjöstrand and Fassbinder adapt it in different ways.

It is well known that the screen, whether big or small, unlike the stage calls for illusionistic presentation. Being a realistic drama with few characters and one setting – important for the small screen – *A Doll's House* lends itself to television presentation. You might even argue that as a realistic play it is today even more suited for the screen than for the stage. Until, say, the 1920s the Helmer living-room tended to be visualised on the stage in a minutely realistic way. With the arrival of film and, later, television – media which can present environments much more realistically – meticulous stage realism gradually gave way to selective realism and even to highly stylised presentations.

This development means that the play's few non-realistic ingredients are now easier to accept on the stage than they were at the time when illusionism held sway in the theatre. While these ingredients no longer present a problem to the stage director, they do to the director of the realistically oriented screen media. The soliloquies of *A Doll's House* is a case in point. Let us see how Nora's thirteen soliloquies are handled in four of the examined teleplays, those by Kehlmann, Sjöstrand, Brinchmann and Thacker.

It is a commonplace to state that especially in the screen media the physical distance between spectator and character implies a mental distance. A Nora who delivers her soliloquies in long shot is not a Nora we easily identify with. Understandably, none of the directors have chosen this solution. They all have Nora soliloquise in close-up, frontally looking at us. Thacker at times even resorts to extreme close-ups.

While Kehlmann and Thacker retain most of the soliloquies, Sjöstrand and Brinchmann omit many of them. Brinchmann, being the most consistent realist of the four directors, frequently replaces the soliloquies with pantomime, making us guess from facial expressions what is on Nora's mind. When he retains a soliloquy he makes it realistically more acceptable by reducing it to a few words. In these pantomimic passages we see 'another Nora, a Nora Helmer has never known. In this way the great scene of transformation – when Nora discards her masquerade costume – was prepared from the first moment.'[4]

All the directors keep the soliloquy that provides a strong curtain for Act II, opening with 'Five o'clock' and concluding with 'Thirty-one hours to live' (seq. 57). In the play text this soliloquy is somewhat loosely motivated by Nora's looking *at her watch*. Sjöstrand here improves on Ibsen. His Nora, standing next to the clock on the mantelpiece, starts to soliloquise about the time left to her as the clock strikes five. Similarly Nora's 'Corrupt my little children!' (seq. 30), by Ibsen not concretely related to anything around Nora, is in Sjöstrand's version motivated by her looking into the nursery at this point. The director even has us share her view of the Helmer children, asleep in their beds – a sentimental touch akin to that of Ibsen's alternative ending.

Kehlmann has Nora utter her soliloquy in sequence 44 standing with her back to one of the doors of the living-room. The position suggests both her anguish about leaving the room for fear of meeting Krogstad and her feeling of being locked up in it, cornered.

Unlike the other directors, Thacker adds soft mood music to a couple of the early soliloquies; flute to the one in sequence 22, strings to the one in sequence 26. The non-diegetic music here serves to underline Nora's development from relative harmony to an increasingly disturbed state of mind. However, this concretisation of the idea that the 'music' gradually disappears out of Nora's life seems both sentimental and trite.

It is, perhaps, surprising that none of the directors has resorted to voice-over, showing us Nora's face with motionless lips in close-up while we hear her soliloquising. The reason may be that voice-over leads to demands on realism which cannot be fulfilled within the constraints of the play text.[5] Laurence Olivier's screen solution for Hamlet's soliloquies means turning them into interior monologues. And the interior monologue tallies neither with Shakespearean blank verse nor with Ibsenite coherent sentence structure. In short, this solution counteracts its own purpose.

Turning to the opening of the play, we come across very different solutions. Falck's script opens with close-ups of small objects:

> *During the credits a pair of hands is seen picking up Christmas decorations from a table – Norwegian union flags, balls, flowers, candle-holders, candles. The decorations are neatly arranged in rows. When the credits are finished, there is a momentary switch to* ANNE-MARIE'S *face, as* NORA *can be heard by the front door.*

> NORA Please put the Christmas tree there in the hall. How much is it?

> ANNE-MARIE *alone in picture, busy with the candles. The voice of a* PORTER. Fifty öre.

> NORA Here's a crown. No, keep it all.

> ANNE-MARIE *shakes her head – lovingly – at this generosity. Then* NORA *enters the room.*

> NORA Hide the Christmas tree carefully, Anne-Marie. The children mustn't see it until tonight when it is decorated.

> ANNE-MARIE *goes to the hall.* NORA *goes to the door by* HELMER'S *study.*[6]

By means of the little flags, the director provides a link between the imbalanced union between Sweden and Norway on the one hand and that of the marital partners on the other, Nora's leaving Helmer anticipating Norway's independence of Sweden, achieved in 1905. The neat arrangement of the Christmas decorations introduces us, as it were, to the aesthetic doll-house world. Nora's generosity is experienced via the Nurse who, rather like Helmer, takes a critical–benevolent attitude to her.

Kehlmann opens with a shot of the stairs in the Helmer apartment house and with happy piano music – as a background for the credits. The choice of instrument relates to the fact that there is a piano in the Helmer living-room, and since the sound of a piano seems quite natural in this kind of environment, the music may well be regarded as diegetic. Nora, loaded with parcels, climbs the stairs, followed by the Porter, carrying a Christmas tree. Kehlmann then cuts to the other side of the apartment door, as it is opened by the Maid. Nora enters, pays the Porter, takes off her fur hat and adjusts her hair in front of the mirror in the hall, merrily humming.

Much more removed from the drama text is the opening in Sjöstrand's version. Helmer is here called Torvald, a cue designation in line with Sjöstrand's inclination to see Helmer as an individual rather than as a pillar of male society. Anxious to adjust the play to the television medium, Sjöstrand divided his script into no fewer than sixty-five different scenes, each scene shift representing a change of place. In the opening section we move with Nora from the Credit Bank (Scenes 1–2), where Helmer has just officially accepted his new post as manager, to a toy shop (3); then to a shop for gloves (4); then back to the bank (5); then to a tea-room (6); then back to the bank again, inside (7–8) and outside (9); and finally to outside the Helmers' apartment house (10). Not until Scene 11 do we find ourselves in the hall, where Ibsen's play begins. Once inside the house we see, in turn, the various rooms of the apartment; besides the living-room and the hall, Helmer's study, the dining-room, the children's room and the kitchen. Towards the end a couple of scenes take place in the street outside. This arrangement was only slightly simplified in the actual production.

It will be seen that Sjöstrand opens his production by cross-cutting between Helmer's masculine world and Nora's feminine one – a contrast that is indicated spatially already in the play text where Rank and Krogstad but not Nora enter Helmer's study.[7] Nora's doll mentality is demonstrated from the very beginning as she listens '*with childish affection*' to her husband's speech (added by Sjöstrand) about 'trustful collaboration' – a speech which seems utterly hypocritical to Krogstad, who has just learnt that he has been dismissed.

An advantage of Sjöstrand's rearrangement is that the meeting between Nora, Mrs Linde and Rank is made more plausible. The two women simply come across each other in the tea-room, where after a while Rank joins them. Nora's secret eating of macaroons is replaced by her revelling in pastries – against her explicit promise to Helmer. Nora brings Mrs Linde from the tea-room to the bank, in the hope that she can persuade Helmer to find a post for her there. From the bank the director cuts to a shot of Nora with her three children on the sofa in the Helmer living-room, the lonely Mrs Linde sitting opposite the happy family.

In Sjöstrand's adaptation not only the initial Porter sequence but also the fairly long 'lark-and-squirrel' passage, which establishes the doll-house relationship between Helmer and Nora, has been replaced by one depicting the social environment to which the Helmer household belongs.

Kjærulff-Schmidt opens his version as follows:

> *The street.* NORA *is on her way home with her three* CHILDREN *and some parcels. They are happy.* NORA *discovers a* MAN *with some Christmas trees on a hand-cart on the other side of the road. The* MAN *is about to unload one of the trees.* NORA *runs away with the* CHILDREN *so that they shall not see anything. They steal into the entrance of the house.*
>
> *The apartment. The hall.* NORA *pushes the* CHILDREN *away to the* NURSE *as the door-bell rings. The* CHILDREN *are gone when* HELENE *opens the door for the* MAN *with the Christmas tree.* NORA *takes out her purse.*
>
> NORA Anne-Marie will help you to take off your clothes and perhaps cut out some things with you . . .
>
> *The* CHILDREN *are gone.* Hide the Christmas tree, Helene! The children must not see it until tonight when it is decorated. *To the* PORTER. How much is it?[8]

Like Sjöstrand, Kjærulff-Schmidt opens his version outside the Helmer apartment. But in his case it is not so much in order to present a social background for the ensuing action. Significantly, the urban environment remains visually somewhat vague in Kjærulff-Schmidt's rather brief initial exterior setting.[9] The purpose of this opening is the more limited one of expanding, and thus emphasising, the theme of hiding indicated in the first speech of the play.

Unlike Sjöstrand and Kjærulff-Schmidt, Brinchmann follows the source text quite faithfully in his opening (figures indicate shots):

1 NORA *in red coat and* PORTER *with Christmas tree outside door.* NORA *rings the bell.*

2 *Close-up of* NORA *through glass of door, from inside. Ringing of bell.*

3 HELMER *at desk in his green-walled study, book in left hand, pen in right. When he hears the bell he smiles, gets up, goes to the door of his room, opens it, looks out.*

4 *The hall and behind it a long corridor. A door in the background is opened and the* MAID *approaches.*

5 HELMER *in door opening waves to the* MAID *with his book, indicating that she should open the door.*

6 MAID *opens front door.* NORA *enters with a basket full of parcels in one hand and a big parcel in the other. Behind her the* PORTER *with the Christmas tree and another basket full of parcels.*
   NORA Hide the Christmas tree away, Helene.

7 *Pan with* NORA *as she moves into the living-room, where she puts down the parcels; turning to the* MAID, *who is still by front door.*
   NORA The children mustn't see it before it is decorated this evening.

8 MAID *and* PORTER *with Christmas tree by front door. The* MAID *takes the tree and basket from the* PORTER *and disappears right.*

9 NORA *up to the* PORTER, *takes out her purse.*
   NORA How much – ?
   PORTER Fifty øre.

> NORA Here's a crown. No, keep it.
> PORTER *thanks her and leaves.* NORA *closes door.*

Within nine shots Ibsen's visualised two-room set (hall and living-room) has been extended with three more areas (exterior, study, corridor). In retrospect the first shot is remarkable in that it is the only exterior shot in the whole teleplay. It clearly relates to the ending, where Nora leaves her doll's house for the world outside.

Already in this brief opening sequence, husband and wife are contrasted visually. *He* is keeping check of the money at his desk. *She* has just been spending a lot of it. Helmer also immediately establishes his role as *paterfamilias*. He knows that Nora is at the front door but it is beneath his dignity to go to the door himself. He orders the Maid to go.

Much like Kehlmann, Thacker opens with a (high angle) shot of Nora and the Porter climbing the staircase as we receive the information about play title and author. But the accompanying string music is in this case decidedly non-diegetic. Here too the camera shifts to the inside of the apartment as we see the Maid open the front door. The Norwegian setting is discreetly indicated as Nora tells the Porter to keep the 'krone'.

In Fassbinder's adapted version entitled *Nora Helmer* – stressing the dehumanising reification of bourgeois society – Nora recklessly makes use of radical feminist slogans to create a comfortable position for herself within a society she claims to fight. The director

> cut all the lines which seemed to her [Margit Carstensen as Nora] most significant and which she most wanted to discuss. He had decided, unilaterally, to show Nora 'as a woman who understands the means she has [at her disposal] to get her own way, to suppress a man. That's what it's about – the man is the victim.'[10]

The power struggle between husband and wife is indicated already in the opening shot, showing Helmer's ringed hand resting upon Nora's shoulder and her ringed hand resting upon his. In this version

9 A remarkably old Krogstad (David Calder) shows Nora (Juliet Stevenson) the signature of her father that she has forged. From the 1991 BBC television version, directed by David Thacker.

of the Helmer marriage Nora clearly has the upper hand. Fassbinder shows the couple, elegantly dressed, separated from one another in a living-room crammed with properties. All the things that the *nouveau riche* couple surround themselves with merely prevent real contact between them.[11] Excelling in glass walls and mirrors, Fassbinder demonstrates how each of them is narcissistically isolated from the other. Characteristically, we rarely see them in two-shot.

One of the visually striking parts of Ibsen's play is the silk-stocking passage:

NORA   ... *(Takes some things out of the box.)* Dr Rank, sit down here and I'll show you something.
RANK *(sits)*   What's this?
NORA   Look here! Look!
RANK   Silk-stockings!
NORA   Flesh-coloured. Aren't they beautiful? It's very dark in here now, of course, but tomorrow – ! No, no, no – only the soles. Oh well, I suppose you can look a bit higher if you want to.
RANK   Hm –
NORA   Why are you looking so critical? Don't you think they'll fit me?
RANK   I can't really give you a qualified opinion on that.
NORA   *(looks at him for a moment)* Shame on you! *(Flicks him on the ear with the stockings.)* Take that. *(Puts them back in the box.)*   *(seq. 39)*

Nora's reprimand to Rank is preceded by a significant acting-direction – *looks at him for a moment* – which could be interpreted in different ways. In earlier performances, it is likely that the short pause implied here would indicate either that Nora does not immediately understand what Rank is hinting at or that she is momentarily speechless, shocked at his remark. In more recent productions it is more likely that she does not *look* at all shocked although she verbally pretends to be.

Kehlmann and Sjöstrand omit the stocking passage. Thacker's Nora merely picks up a small paper parcel, unrolls a flesh-coloured silk-stocking and shows it to Rank. After his remark, she flicks him on the nose with the stocking. Brinchmann's Nora, far from being upset by Rank's remark, seems quite amused at it. None of the directors, we must conclude, makes much of the silk-stocking passage.

The tarantella sequences (seq. 52–3) are difficult to do on the small screen. Nora needs some space for her dancing. Moreover, at the end of this passage we have three other characters spread out in the room: Rank '*at the piano*', Helmer '*by the stove*', and Mrs Linde '*in the doorway*'. While on the stage Nora's state of mind at this point will be illuminated by her wild dancing, in a TV version such kinesics may, in part, be replaced by mimicry. To what extent does the director want to show the dancing and to what extent does (s)he want to show Nora's facial expressions while dancing? To what extent, in other words, does (s)he opt for long shots, medium shots, close-ups? What does (s)he focus on? Nora's anguish? The 'master–slave' relationship between Helmer and Nora? The bond – by love and death – between Nora and Rank? Or all of these things?

Kehlmann shows Nora in long shot, the piano in the foreground. Helmer here guides his wife by dancing himself.

Brinchmann begins the tarantella with a long shot of Nora, tambourine in hand, then cuts to a shot showing Helmer at the piano in the foreground and Nora dancing in the background. In a series of shots – in which the camera gradually comes closer to Nora without actually reaching close-up distance – the director focuses on Nora's increasingly wild dance and the mimicry that goes with it.

Sjöstrand aborts such a climactic development by opting for cross-cutting. From the tarantella he cuts to a shot showing how Mrs Linde in vain visits Krogstad. Cutting back to the tarantella he then shows how Helmer rather emphatically instructs Nora. The passage ends with Nora throwing the tambourine to Mrs Linde.

Thacker, finally, switches back and forth between long shots of the room, two-shots of Helmer instructing Nora, and shots showing Nora's face in the foreground, Helmer and Rank in the background. Somewhat surprisingly, Mrs Linde enters in the foreground left. Carefully designed, there is nevertheless a lack of focus in Thacker's rather theatrical handling of the tarantella.

10 Lise Fjeldstad as Nora in her Neapolitan tarantella costume,
tambourine in hand. From the Norwegian 1974 television
production, directed by Arild Brinchmann.

The highly symbolic cigar-lighting in sequence 67 loses all significance in Sjöstrand's version. The director has Helmer rather than
Nora light Rank's cigar, and he omits Nora's and Rank's metaphoric
references to the fire.

With Brinchmann it is a rather slow, intimate passage. We see, in close-up, the flame of Nora's match lighting Rank's long cigar. The medium here helps to clarify the sexual connotations. Rank's leave-taking is done as follows:

Close up of NORA. Sleep well, Dr Rank.
Medium shot of RANK *who turns around to face her.* Thanks...
Close-up of NORA. Wish me the same!
Close-up of RANK. Sleep well. And thanks for the fire.

Thacker's Rank asks Helmer for a cigar, seemingly to get him out of the way, so that he can be alone with Nora. After a close-up of Nora and Rank, showing her lighting his cigar to the accompaniment of non-diegetic theme music, Helmer appears in the background between the two – an obstacle and an outsider.

For Rank's departure, Thacker again places Helmer in the background, this time by the apartment entrance, impatiently waiting for Rank to leave. Nora is in the foreground. Rank, midway between the two, looks at Nora, and us, as he says 'Sleep well. And thanks for the light.' The long shot arrangement at this point makes a rather theatrical impression.

Returning from the Stenborg party, Helmer, intoxicated by the champagne, demands his 'matrimonial rights':

HELMER ... When I saw you dance the tarantella, like a huntress, a temptress, my blood grew hot, I couldn't stand it any longer! That was why I seized you and dragged you down here with me –
    NORA Leave me, Torvald! Get away from me! I don't want all this.
HELMER What? Now, Nora, you're joking with me. Don't want, don't want – ? Aren't I your husband?
(There is a knock on the front door.)   *(seq.65)*

The 'seduction' is interrupted by Rank's appearance. The dialogue implies, of course, that Helmer is close to Nora at this point. But is he behaving 'gentlemanly' or not? Is he softly pleading or brutally demanding? The director has a range of options here.

While Ibsen's Helmer does not even kiss his wife at this moment – he has just kissed her '*on the forehead*' – Sjöstrand's Helmer unbuttons her around the neck and kisses her with increasing intensity. Even so he is a rather quiet seducer. What is more, Sjöstrand's Nora, still accepting her conjugal obligations, gives way and returns her husband's kisses.

Brinchmann's Helmer is much more violent. Taking off Nora's bodice, pressing her breasts, putting his hand under her skirt and forcing himself between her legs, this Helmer is actually raping his wife when Rank's knock interrupts him.

Thacker's Helmer is even more violent. Performing much the same actions as Brinchmann's, he does it in a sadistic rather than voluptuous manner. When the knock is heard, he points an authoritarian finger at Nora, telling her to arrange her clothes and make herself presentable. The gap between appearances and reality is strongly emphasised.

Brinchmann and Thacker both demonstrate the ugliness behind the proper matrimonial façade. Rather than titillate the spectator or update the play, their presentations of the seduction have an emblematic function similar to the one we have found in Bergman's handling of the monetary passage, the rape being an extreme sign of male dominance. But while such an emblematic approach seems fitting for the stylised medium of the stage, it is doubtful if it suits the realistic television medium.

As could be expected, the ending of the play has been done very differently. When Kehlmann's Nora, having shifted to the suit costume she wore in the beginning, utters the closing words of the play, she and Helmer are still in the living-room:

Medium close-up of HELMER's *neck left and of* NORA's *face, in semi-profile, right, looking at him.*
NORA *matter-of-factly.* That our life together could become a marriage. *Looks down, softly.* Goodbye. *Turns away and moves towards the door in the background.*

She opens the door and disappears. Along with Helmer we stare at the closed door. He then shouts 'Nora!', runs to the door, opens it, rushes to the balcony of the stairs outside the apartment, looks down the stairs and shouts again: 'Nora!' He then moves back into the apartment, looks at her ring in his open hand, begins to laugh the laugh of a drunkard or a madman, and sits down by the table. As his head falls down on it, he seems to lose consciousness. Music starts as the camera pans to the right and takes in part of the floor. There is not even a glimmer of hope in this ending – without a door slam – suggesting that Helmer is completely incapable of coping with the situation.

In Sjöstrand's script version the end reads as follows:

63 ...

NORA That our life together could become – a marriage. Goodbye.

64 NORA *leaves the house.* TORVALD *remains standing where he was for a long time, completely still. Then he starts to move, aimlessly, bewildered, and as he now begins to understand what has really happened, he gives way to a genuine desperation. Suddenly he goes to the window, opens it and shouts.* Nora!

65 *The Street.*

NORA *moves away.* TORVALD'S *voice echoes between the walls of the houses.* Nora! Nora!

She turns around but does not stop. The picture of her face is frozen.

Here the final shot – of Nora, not of Helmer – is a subjective one, expressing the idea that the memory of her will stay with him – a visual counterpart of the play text's call for a dawning hope. However, in the actual production the script was not followed to the letter; a transcription of the ending as transmitted might read:

NORA, *wearing a white shawl, and* TORVALD *in the hall by the front door. Slightly high-angle medium close-up of* TORVALD'S *neck left and* NORA'S *neck right. (She is facing the door.) She turns around, looks at him, smiles vaguely.*

> NORA *almost pertly.* That our life together could become a marriage. *Turns toward the door, opens it and leaves.*
>
> TORVALD *remains by the door for a while, then walks slowly back into the living-room, all the time fingering the ring he has just got back from her. Quietly desperate he says to himself.* Nora. *Then goes to the window, opens it and shouts.* Nora! Nora! *The name reverberates along the street. Fade-out.*

As with Kehlmann, Nora here wears the same costume she wore in the beginning of the play. Only the shawl, an ironical veil or a shroud, is added. Since there is no travelling-bag to be seen, Nora's departure seems rather rash. Along with other signifiers – notably the positive way in which her husband is depicted – it contributes to our impression that this Nora is likely to return.

As in the play text, the final focus is on Helmer. His walking through the large living-room accentuates his feeling of loneliness, the emptiness of his present existence. His desperation is expressed by his calling for his wife in the middle of the night. We are here a long way from the man who is afraid of making a scandal.

Brinchmann's Nora at the end puts on a brown coat with black-fur trimmings – instead of the black shawl called for in the text. She does not pick up the suitcase until immediately before leaving. Standing by the front door of the apartment, she utters her exit line:

> *Straight-on close-up of* NORA, *looking down.*
> NORA *hesitantly.* That . . . our life together could become . . . a marriage.
> *Pause. Turns towards the door.* Goodbye.

Helmer runs after her as she leaves through the cross-shaped glass-and-wood apartment door. Her steps can be heard as she walks down the stairs. Helmer turns, closes the door, looks at the ring she has returned to him, walks back into the living-room and says, 'Empty'. He sits down in the middle of the sofa, a position empha-sising his loneliness, and mumbles puzzled, 'The most wonderful thing?' '*Faint door slam. Fade-out.*'

In Fassbinder's ending Nora's final line has, significantly, been cut.[12] Moreover, Nora's change to a dressing-gown is a sign that she does not leave. The room has been cleared of all the properties that crammed it in the beginning. As the masks have been dropped, the distance between the couple has merely become more obvious.

For the key line Thacker places Nora and Helmer in the living-room, between the table and the piano. She has put on her black coat, he is in the same dark-green smoking-jacket he wore in the beginning. We then get:

> *Straight-on close-up of* NORA *left and* HELMER *right, both in profile, looking at one another. While the light of daybreak is faintly seen on her face, his face is slightly turned away so that we cannot see his eyes.*
>
> NORA *softly but insistently gesticulating.* Change so much that our life together ... could become a marriage. *Soft, melancholy string music starts and continues until the end.*
>
> NORA *still looking at* HELMER, *very softly.* Goodbye. *Looks down, turns away.*

She then moves toward the door and the camera so that we, unlike Helmer, can see her face at the moment of departure. After a close-up of Helmer, pathetically crying, Thacker has him shout 'Nora!' while rushing after her out onto the staircase. Looking down the stairs, he whispers 'Empty', then returns slowly to the apartment. We see his face in close-up, on the verge of tears but with a trembling smile on his lips, as he says: 'The most wonderful thing of all?' The final shot of the empty staircase as the door slam is heard reveals that Thacker was more interested in presenting an ironical circle compo-sition – the opening and closing shots of the staircase are identical – than in showing Helmer's reaction to the door slam.

Thacker's ending is problematic. While Ibsen's Helmer meaning-fully experiences the matrimonial apartment as 'empty', Thacker's rather pointlessly experiences the collective staircase as such. The idea of having the melancholy music follow directly upon the key line means sentimentalising Nora's statement. And the combination of a lonely, pathetic Helmer, in close-up, and this kind of 'mood music' results in a rather trite ending.

CHAPTER 7

'A DOLL'S HOUSE' AS FILM

The unity of time and place, the limited number of characters and the emphasis on the verbal component – all these aspects which favour adaptations for radio and television, would appear to be far from positive factors when we turn to the film medium. Here precisely the opposite seems desirable: frequent changes of environment, a great number of minor characters and extras, emphasis on the visual.

Yet *A Doll's House* has proved to be very popular with film-makers. By 1978 the play had been filmed no less than twelve times. Five of the films were produced in the United States.

Just as two versions of the ending were presented in the early German stage productions, so Berthold Viertel offered two versions in his 1922/3 silent film, one with an ending in agreement with that of the play, the other more in agreement with Ibsen's conciliatory alternative ending. The latter ending was again resorted to in Harald Braun's heavily adapted 1944 version, set in Holstein, where the couple are finally united by Helmer's mother.[1]

In the American 1922 version,

> Nazimova attempted both faithfulness to Ibsen's script and at the
> same time exploitation of the camera. The film begins with the early
> married life of Nora and Torvald. Much of the off-stage action is
> shown on the screen. One of the finest moments was Krogstad's first
> entrance. Nora is playing with her children and everything is happy
> until the ominous shadow of Krogstad appears on the door, indicat-
> ing a new threat to the peace and joy of the home. When Nora
> returns after seeing him out, she finds the house in pandemonium:
> the baby is crying, one of the children is banging on the piano, and

another is trying to break a music box. They all howl when their mother tries to restore order. The scene foreshadows the ruin of the bigger world in which she is living.[2]

Much later, in 1973, an English version, directed by Patrick Garland, was released. Based on a stage production, Garland's film is rather theatrical and seems better suited for television transmission than for the large screen. More adapted to the big screen is Joseph Losey's French–English version, also produced in 1973 and first shown on television. In the following I shall limit myself to these two relatively recent versions, which demonstrate two main options offered to those who wish to turn a play written for the stage into a film. On the one hand, there is the cinematic approach – in which case much of the dialogue has to be cut, a considerable problem when you are dealing with such a dense text as that of *A Doll's House*. On the other, there is the verbose, theatrical one, in which case you do not do justice to the film medium.

If we regard film as a mainly realistic medium, inimical to wordiness, then it is not surprising that Nora's soliloquies, which are partly retained in the examined radio and television versions, are omitted both by Garland and Losey. Another difference is that film tends to resort more to non-diegetic mood music than radio and television drama. While Garland uses music sparsely, Losey rather tiringly has sombre brass music, leitmotif fashion, accompany most of the exterior scenes. Since a brass band is precisely what we might expect to find in a little Norwegian town, you might say that Losey handles diegetic music in a non-diegetic way.

In his film, Garland shows us little of the world outside the Helmer apartment. And the apartment in a film, Bazin assures us, feels even more cramped than a room on the stage.[3] Actually, the Helmers in Garland's version live not in an apartment at all but in a (doll's) house, and we listen to English Christmas carols rather than to Scandinavian Christmas hymns. In short, the environment seems more British than Norwegian. By contrast, Losey eagerly incorporates the nineteenth-century environment surrounding the Helmer apartment in his version, shot on location in the little mining town of Røros, Norway.

In a film, Nora can be shown more fully and more convincingly in the outside world than in the most heavily adapted, multi-set stage version. In this sense Losey's presentation seems influenced by his medium. Like Sjöstrand, he 'breaks up the theatrical time/space continuum by setting the action in a variety of locations and by cross-cutting among them for dramatic emphasis and tension'.[4] However, Losey's use of the film medium is in conflict with a major theme of the play. Ibsen's unity of setting strengthens our feeling that Nora is a prisoner in her own house. Her final exit seems so definite not least because it is the first time that we see her leave her doll's house. In Losey's film this essential aspect is diluted by the romantic exterior shots of the beautiful wooden houses of Røros, of turn-of-the-century horse-sleighs, and of skating men and women. Losey has, in fact, replaced the doll's house by a doll town, making both Nora and Helmer victims of its bourgeois morals.

The same expanding tendency, Hirsch notes, is found in Losey's version of the Helmer apartment, which shows

> a series of rooms that open into one another, so that there is a sense of deep and receding space; behind the living room can be seen the dining room; on the other side of the stairs from Nora's bedroom is the children's room – the physical separation between Nora and her children, the children glimpsed in the rear of the frame with their nurse, makes a telling point about Nora's distance from them.

There is little of Ibsen's confining living-room in this spacious apartment which is

> sedate, heavy, utterly ordered and dignified: nothing is out of place in these rich and elegant rooms; . . . The apartment, in short, looks nothing like a doll's house, being clearly the residence of very sober and well-off adults. There is no sign of Nora in these stiff and beautifully appointed rooms, no expression of her lightheartedness and charm. The mise-en-scène makes her seem like a stranger in her own house . . . [5]

Like many other critics, Hirsch here seems to assume that Ibsen's living-room is designed according to Nora's rather than Helmer's taste. But as we have seen, this is not the case. Losey's design of the Helmer residence is therefore merely strengthening what is suggested in the stage-directions: that the Helmer apartment is dominated by male aesthetics. By turning Nora into 'a stranger in her own house' Losey to some extent wins back what he has lost by letting her out of her doll's house long before she definitely steps out of it.

With regard to costume, Garland's Nora appears first in a dark blue dress (Act I), then in a green one (Act II). At the end she changes from Neapolitan folk costume to a brown travelling dress. Losey's Nora, too, appears in a blue dress in the early part of the film, later in black. Her Capri costume has a black top, covered by a white shawl, a red skirt and a white apron. At the end – after Losey has cross-cut to a scene between Krogstad and Mrs Linde – she appears again in her blue dress, now with a black shawl around her shoulders. While Ibsen's Nora changes from fancy-dress to everyday clothes in a very emphatic way, with Losey the change is almost unnoticeable.

Garland opens his version with an establishing-shot, the only explicit outdoor shot in the whole film:

1 NORA *behind a* COACHMAN *in a horse-sleigh riding through a snowy landscape. Jingling of sleigh-bells. Music-box music. Children throwing snowballs at the sleigh, which continues into town.*

2 *A front door (from inside). Ringing of doorbell. A* MAID *opens the door, which has a Christmas garland on it, and lets in* NORA, *who carries a lot of parcels, including a doll's bed. Music-box music.*

NORA Is Mr Helmer in?
MAID Yes, ma'am.

The romantic initial shot serves several functions. It introduces us to the protagonist, Nora, as a passive passenger next to an active male, taking her from the countryside (nature) into the town (society/

culture). Somewhere in between they are attacked by the children. The diegetic sound of the sleigh-bells contrasts with the non-diegetic one of the doll-like music-box. In this opening shot the dilemma Nora is soon to experience is presented metaphorically.

Losey's film opens with a pre-title sequence, taking us back to the pre-scenic events of the play. A few establishing shots inform us that the time is approximately the one indicated by Ibsen. Men and women (in long dresses) are skating; there are horse-sleighs with bells. Nora and Mrs Linde take off their skates and enter a coffeehouse by the skating-rink. We learn that Nora is getting married to Helmer within a week, while Mrs Linde has been forced to dismiss Krogstad for a husband with a secure income. This prologue outlines the contrasting situations in which the two women find themselves, one joining a man, the other leaving one. The irony is that, despite leaving Krogstad, Mrs Linde is truly in love with him, while Nora, despite marrying Helmer, seems more in love with the status and prospects he offers than with Helmer himself. In this way Losey, unlike Ibsen, interprets the past for us and makes us side with Mrs Linde rather than Nora from the very beginning.

After the credits, we are introduced to the urban environment. We witness Nora, pregnant, and Rank, the doctor, next to her dying father; the Helmers' departure for Italy and their return from there; the interior of the Credit Bank and of a tea-room; we accompany Nora as she is buying Christmas presents and a Christmas tree. For some of these scenes Losey comes exceedingly close to Sjöstrand's television adaptation.

In his presentation of the tarantella, Garland frequently cross-cuts between Nora's dancing and Mrs Linde's visit to Krogstad. This suggests, in a rather obvious, medium-oriented way, what is on Nora's mind while she is dancing. Toward the end of the tarantella, the director cuts – via two close-ups of Nora's face – from the rehearsal to the actual performance of the tarantella at the fancy-dress ball upstairs, thereby indicating a time lapse. Cross-cutting is again used to contrast Helmer and Nora, miles apart although dancing together,

11 Unlike Ibsen, Patrick Garland, in his 1973 film version, shows us
Nora's performance at the Stenborg fancy-dress ball. Mrs Linde
and Helmer unmask themselves as they watch Nora (Claire
Bloom) dancing her tarantella.

with Krogstad and Mrs Linde, who are finding their way back to one another. At the same time close-ups of Nora's legs recall the erotic silk-stocking scene, in which Rank's secret love for Nora was revealed.

The erotic emphasis is also found in Losey's film – although the connection with the silk-stocking scene is missing there. Nora in dark blue rehearses a wild tarantella. Helmer objects with words added in the screenplay: 'There's a difference between a dance and a wanton display.' In protest, Nora then starts to dance can-can fashion, very obviously siding with Rank. This provocative Nora is a rather far cry from Ibsen's heroine, who at this point is torn between opposing loyalties. As for the musical element, the tarantella is especially appropriate in Garland's version, since it is there an echo, in the minor, of the music-box tune with which the film began.

No doubt the erotic emphasis in the two films has something to do with the casting of an attractive star as Nora, and the ease with which the film medium can offer titillating close-ups. Actually, considering the subtlety with which Claire Bloom portrays her, Garland's Nora is psychologically rather than erotically exciting. By comparison Losey's Nora, who had to make do with a banal, all-too-explicit version of Ibsen's dialogue, seems rather lacking in nuances.

While Losey omits the silk-stocking, the cigar-lighting and the seduction scene, Garland retains them all. In the silk-stocking scene (seq. 39), Rank is only allowed to see the foot. He lowers his eyes. Nora holds up the stocking and Rank touches it. When Rank a little later tells Nora of his love for her, Ibsen's Nora moves to the doorway and asks the Maid to bring in the lamp. This is clearly her excuse for moving away from the doctor who is becoming too intimate. Similarly, Garland's Nora moves away from Rank to fetch fire from the fire-place. Lighting the lamp, she reproaches him for his outspokenness. Her action – anticipating the cigar-lighting scene – can be seen as a symbolic gesture in line with the verbal *double-entendres* the two exchange, indicating that she secretly returns Rank's love.

In the seduction scene (seq. 65) Garland has a tender Helmer

12 Joseph Losey, too, in his 1973 film version, shows us Nora (Jane Fonda) dancing the tarantella at the Stenborg party.

bring Nora to bed. He kisses her dearly and, unlike Ibsen's Nora, Garland's is about to give way when Rank's knocking interrupts their love-making.

In the cigar-lighting scene (seq. 67), Nora lights Rank's cigar while Helmer watches them. She then walks with Rank to the door. Helmer is now out of sight. In the next long shot we see Rank walking alone to the door where Helmer is waiting to let him out. Rank turns round and says loudly to Nora who, unseen in the foreground, occupies the same place as the spectator: 'And thanks for the light.'

The theatrical manner in which this passage is filmed suggests that it has been carried over from the stage version without any significant change. Since Rank's love declaration to Nora, thanking her for 'the fire' (as the source text has it), is here uttered aloud as it would be on the stage, the impression is that the intention of the *double-entendre* is to disclose something to Nora and at the same time keep Helmer ignorant. Garland sticks to this stagey solution rather than have Rank utter these words close to Nora, so that only she can hear them. This might have been an alternative option in a screen version, indicating that Rank wants to keep the meaning of the words disguised even for Nora, who has earlier blamed him for being too outspoken in this matter.

At the end of Garland's film Helmer and Nora, both in black, are seen by the front door of the apartment. As Nora leaves, we see the door with a Christmas garland (!) on it closing. A long shot shows Helmer walking back through the extensive, narrow hall – a way of making him seem small and lonely – into the living-room, where he stops. There is no need for him to say 'Empty', as Ibsen's Helmer does, since another long shot of the big living-room visualises his feelings. There is a slow zoom-in to an extreme close-up of his face as he says, 'The most wonderful miracle'. Then comes the sound of the street door slamming shut, crushing his hope. Fade-out and, as an ironical footnote, sweet, doll-like, non-diegetic music, as from a music-box – the kind of music that was heard at the beginning of the film.

In Losey's film the last speech is Nora's 'We would have to change so much . . . '. Having said this, she puts on a black coat and leaves quickly, without saying goodbye. Helmer remains standing in the living-room. When he hears her slam the street door shut, he lowers his head. Even when left alone, he performs a social ritual. There is a shot of the fatal letter-box, now open, and a final exterior shot of the church in the distance, swept in mist and snow. The chiming of the church bells mingles with the sombre brass music that has been heard intermittently throughout the film – two sounds expressing the power of the religious, bourgeois society of which Helmer and Nora have become victims.

CHAPTER 8

TRANSPOSING THE END
OF 'A DOLL'S HOUSE'

When analysing drama performances in the widest sense of the word, it seems sensible to distribute the enormous amount of signifiers transmitted to the recipient (the spectator and/or the listener) over five *codes*: (1) language, (2) culture, (3) medium, (4) directorial and (5) actorial signals.

Each of these five codes can be related to a number of *sign categories*. Kowzan, concerned only with live performances, distinguishes thirteen such categories,[1] Fischer-Lichte adds one more.[2] Esslin, dealing with both stage and screen performances, discerns five 'sign systems common to all dramatic media' and another three confined to cinema and television.[3] Although Esslin's wider scope coincides with the one applied here, his somewhat unsystematic classification seems problematic. Granted that any classification suffers from overlapping and borderline cases, the following combination of the three schemes just referred to seems helpful for a comparative approach to performance analysis:

Text, stage and screen categories
1　play area
2　scenery
3　properties
4　lighting
5　sound
6　music
7　physical constitution
8　mimicry
9　kinesics

10 proxemics

11 make-up

12 costume

13 paralinguistics

14 dialogue

Screen categories

15 camera work

16 linking of shots (editing)

When comparing different performances of the same play, we need to break down each of them into comparable parts for analysis. In many cases changes in character constellation will here be a determinant factor. But a division into sequences will hardly be enough. Within the sequences we may distinguish shorter units, *segments*, where demarcation lines are based on topical shifts.[4] In each segment many of the sign categories listed in the classification scheme will appear.

Next to such a 'vertical' analysis, we may deal 'horizontally' with each one of the sign categories.[5] A property, a lighting effect, a costume, a gesture, a sound, a phrase, a camera angle will often be meaningful not only when combined vertically with other signifiers in the immediate context but also when combined horizontally with related signifiers in other parts of the play text and/or performance text.

By focusing on how the ending of *A Doll's House* has been rendered in translations and performances discussed earlier, we shall now, by way of conclusion, see how a comparative approach to performance analysis can illuminate the relationship between constants and variables in the performance text, defined as the totality of signs employed in a production.

The productions that concern us are, again, those of the following nine directors:

Stage
Neuenfels, Frankfurt 1972

Saari, Gothenburg 1985
Bergman, Stockholm 1989

Television
Kehlmann, West Germany 1961
Sjöstrand, Sweden 1970
Brinchmann, Norway 1974
Thacker, England 1991

Film
Garland, England 1973
Losey, England/France 1973

In one case (Brinchmann) we deal with the source text, albeit in modernised form. In the other cases we deal with target texts, either Swedish (Sjöstrand, Saari, Bergman), German (Kehlmann, Neuenfels) or English (Garland, Losey, Thacker). The difference between source and target text is of great significance both with regard to the effect it has on the recipient and with regard to the director's choice of non-linguistic signifiers.

A considerable problem when comparing stage and screen performances of any sizeable play is, as we have noted before, that the dialogue of screen versions – especially those for the big screen – tends to be considerably shorter than that of stage versions. Yet there is no hard and fast rule. Thus, Brinchmann's television version, which runs close to two hours, actually retains more of Ibsen's dialogue than Bergman's heavily cut stage version. In fact, the presentations discussed here all retain different amounts and, to some extent, different parts of the source dialogue.

The questions which the comparative performance semiotician may ask are, for example: How do the nine directors handle signs which have been provided explicitly or implicitly in the drama text? And to what extent do the productions differ from one another because of variations with regard to the linguistic, cultural, medial, directorial or actorial code?

One of the central symbols of the play, we have earlier observed, is the Christmas tree. *Culturally*, the Christmas tree is both geographically and historically determined; geographically, since in non-Christian parts of the world it is a strange, more or less unintelligible phenomenon; historically, since few recipients today realise that a Christmas tree around 1880 was a status symbol, an indication that you belonged to the better situated in society.

The Christmas tree is referred to already in the first speech of the play, where Nora states:

> Hide the Christmas tree away carefully, Helene. The children mustn't see it till this evening when it's decorated.

With regard to the *language*, that is, through the enunciated signs of the performance text, we are here informed that it is Christmas Eve – provided we assume that this is traditionally the day in Norway on which the Christmas tree is decorated. Already in the first speech of the play Ibsen suggests, by his choice of the word 'pyntet' (decorated), a correspondence between the Christmas tree and Nora. Unfortunately, the connection is obscured in the target texts, where Mrs Linde, for idiomatic reasons, wishes to see Nora 'all dressed up' (McFarlane), 'in her costume' (Meyer, Watts) or 'in costume' (Fjelde).

From a *media* point of view, the Christmas tree in the text would obviously differ from one on the stage and both would again differ from a tree in a television or film version – not to mention a radio version, where the tree would hardly be noticeable. In the theatre we would have the tree before us throughout the play, while in a television or film version we would see it only incidentally. While its colour would be obvious in a stage version, it would be obscured in a black-and-white television or film presentation.

The *directorial* code is employed by Ibsen himself. In the stage directions for Act II we read:

(*In the corner by the piano the Christmas tree stands, stripped and dishevelled, its candles burned to their sockets.*)

Ibsen here prescribes where the Christmas tree should be placed and what it looks like both at this moment and, since this is the last reference to the tree, until the end of the play. In a performance Ibsen's verbal signifiers will necessarily be transformed into audiovisual ones. Ironically, the playwright's mentioning here of small objects means that his stage-directions at this point are, in fact, more functional for the (not intended) screen than for the (intended) stage. The information provided by Ibsen will necessarily be supplemented by more specific visual information in a performance, such as the size of the tree, its exact colour, its surroundings.

By the *actorial* code is meant the signifiers inherent in the individual actor or actress independent of the part (s)he is performing at the moment: physical constitution, habits of speaking, gesticulating, etc. If we accept the idea that the Christmas tree represents Nora, then it will make a difference whether we have a tall Nora standing next to a small Christmas tree, a small Nora next to a tall tree, or a Nora of the same height as the tree next to her. And what about Nora herself? The question of looks is certainly of paramount importance. Although tastes differ, there is, we may assume, a certain amount of common agreement. An attractive Nora versus an unattractive Helmer creates a situation very different from that of an attractive Nora versus an attractive Helmer. (Another possibility – an unattractive Nora versus an attractive Helmer – would be an odd choice, considering Helmer's aesthetic and social concerns.) The distribution of attractive or unattractive actors/actresses is certainly one of the most effective ways in which a director can manipulate an audience.

Let us now see how the sixteen sign categories listed before are realised at the end of the play.

The term *play area* refers (a) to the proxemic relation between the area where the play is acted out and the audience, and (b) to the homogeneity of the setting. With regard to (a) we may note that in the case of television, the recipient can choose his distance to the screen – as he cannot in the theatre or the cinema. In a stage version, the play area may be separated from the audience according to the naturalistic fourth-wall-gone principle or the audience may surround the play area, arena fashion. In the latter case there will be an uneven distribution and reception of mimicry, since the actors cannot continually turn their faces to all the spectators. In Bergman's Stockholm production there was a more specific reason, relating to the play area. The director here tried to diminish the barrier between actors and spectators by letting the *art nouveau* decor of the auditorium be mirrored in that of the stage scenery.

With regard to (b) Ibsen opts for a unity of setting; throughout the play we find ourselves in the Helmer living-room. Eight of the directors adhere to Ibsen's idea that the leave-taking takes place either in the living-room or in the adjacent hall. The exception is Bergman, who toward the end moves the action from the living-room to the marital bedroom, to bring the play closer to our time, the implication being not only that Nora and Helmer have spent the night in bed together but also that the bedroom and its associations with sexual communion, beginning with the wedding night, is a more painful place to situate a divorce than the living-room or the hall.

Media differences would often account for different styles in *scenery*. In the television and film versions the scenery is realistic while in the stage versions – especially that by Neuenfels – it is more stylised. The period selected agrees in nearly all the cases with the one in the drama text: around 1880. But Neuenfels gives no clear indication of period. And Bergman updates the play to early twentieth century.

Thacker uses a discrete *lighting* effect when he has Nora's face illuminated as she pronounces the key sentence of the play. More striking are Neuenfels' device of having the ending of the play paradoxically set in daylight and Bergman's of having Helmer unmasked in a cold, white 'x-ray' light.

With regard to *costume*, Ibsen prescribes '*ydertøy*' for Nora toward the end of the play. The word literally means 'outdoor clothes' and this is also the rendering used by several translators. Since it is winter, the word may be taken to mean not only coat but also hat; this is confirmed a few lines later when Nora '*ties on her hat*'. When Fjelde translates '*ydertøy*' with '*coat*' and omits Ibsen's explicit reference to the hat, he exceeds his task as a translator. It is another matter that most directors today willingly dispense with the hat.

Besides hat and coat, Ibsen prescribes '*a large black shawl*' for Nora. Shortly before her exit, Nora '*pulls her shawl round her*' – a mournful *gesture*, indicating that this is no frivolous separation.

Since Ibsen does not specify the style or colour of either coat or hat, directors here have free hands. Although Nora is costumed differently in each of the nine versions, most directors have Nora exit in a black coat without a hat. The lack of a hat may be seen as a – hardly noticeable – cultural shift, geographically and/or historically. Garland has her leave in a black, spangled coat – a starry sky? In the foreground we see the contrasting red coat which Nora wore when she entered her home in the beginning. Brinchmann chooses a brown, opulent-looking coat with black-fur trimmings. In Bergman's version Nora wears a simple, timeless black coat, indicating her universal and anonymous representativity. Sjöstrand's Nora, in a black coat of the period, throws a thin, white lace shawl over her head – an ironical bridal veil.

Helmer's costume offers less variation. Ibsen prescribes '*evening dress, with a black domino open over it*'. Bergman shows him returning from the Stenborg party in a red domino and a red jester's cap and half-mask; in the final bedroom scene the mask is hanging next to the nude Helmer, barely 'masked' under the red bed-cover. Garland provides Helmer with too short trousers to underline his immaturity.

The *make-up* may help indicate the time of action in the performance text. Characteristic of the 1880s was that men – Ibsen being one of them – wore a beard and whiskers. Losey's and especially Thacker's Helmer look in this respect decidedly nineteenth century – as Bergman's does not.

A striking example of *dialogue* is found in Nora's last speech, containing one of the most important lines in the whole play. Let us now see how this key line, so difficult to render in English, has been recreated in the nine performances. Two of the directors (Saari, Losey) solve the problem simply by omitting it. In the remaining seven versions the key line appears in the following audiovisual contexts (I disregard the costumes which have been discussed earlier):

(In the living room.) Medium close-up of HELMER's *neck left and of* NORA's *face, in semi-profile right, looking at him.* NORA *matter-of-factly.* That our life together could become a marriage. *Looks down, softly.* Goodbye. *Turns away and moves towards the door in the background.* (Kehlmann)

(In the hall by the front door.) Medium, slightly high-angle close-up of HELMER's *neck left,* NORA's *neck right. (She is facing the door.) She turns around, looks at him, smiles vaguely.*
NORA *almost pertly.* That our life together could become a marriage. *Turns towards the door.* (Sjöstrand)

(In the middle of the huge living-room, dominated by a large window, behind which the blue sky is seen.) NORA, *sitting on the floor, embraces* HELMER *who is kneeling next to her, her blue bag of macaroons in her left hand held against his back.*
NORA *softly but insistently.* Then we would have to change so much that our life together became a marriage. *They stand up and are now seen in profile, facing one another in front of the window.*
NORA *loudly and matter-of-factly.* Goodbye. (Neuenfels)

(In the hall.) Medium straight-on close-up of NORA, *looking at* HELMER.
NORA *softly.* That our life together would become a marriage. *Looks down, takes a step past him.* Goodbye, Torvald. *Moves on past him towards the door (and the camera).* (Garland)

(In the hall by the front door.) Straight-on close-up of NORA *looking down.*

NORA *hesitantly.* That . . . our life together could become . . . a marriage. *Pause. Turns towards the door.* Goodbye. (*Brinchmann*)

(In the bedroom.) NORA, *the travelling-bag next to her, is standing in the shade to the left.* HELMER, *starkly lit, is sitting to the right under the red cover of the white double bed. She turns away from him, wipes her eyes with her handkerchief, picks up her travelling-bag, turns around and looks at him.*

NORA *warmly but firmly.* That our marriage became a life together. *Pause. Turns away.* Goodbye. (*Bergman*)

Straight-on close-up of NORA *left and* HELMER *right, both in profile, looking at one another. While the light of daybreak is seen on her face, his face is slightly turned away so that we cannot see his eyes.*

NORA *softly but insistently gesticulating.* Change so much that our life together . . . could become a marriage. *Soft, melancholy string music begins.*

NORA *very softly, still looking at* HELMER. Goodbye. *Looks down, turns away.* (*Thacker*).

While Nora's key line in six of the versions more or less agrees with the phrasing in the source text, Bergman radically changes it simply by making the two key words change places. As a result the two words receive the weight they have in present-day gender relations. Nora's key line is, as it were, synchronised with the ethical reference frame of a modern audience.

As is natural, Bergman's couple are much farther apart than are those of the screen directors. The media code here supersedes the directorial one. With regard to *proxemics* television, unlike stage and film, demands short distances between the actors. In addition to this media-determined kind of proxemics, Neuenfels may exemplify another one, determined by directorial choice, when he makes Nora and Helmer sit on the floor to indicate their childlike nature, underlined also by the reappearance of the macaroon bag.

While the *kinesics* – gestures and movements – in most versions are realistic, with Neuenfels they are exceedingly stylised, emblematic – as though we are witnessing a series of *tableaux vivants*. Bergman here settles for a middle way. On the one hand, he retains a realistic superstructure, so that the spectators can identify with the characters. At the same time he carefully choreographs all gestures and movements, not least in relation to the speeches, to ensure due attention to the subtext. The result is a rhythmically and 'didactically' orchestrated performance.

What kinesics do for the stage, *mimicry* does for the screen. Notably in the high-quality close-ups of the big screen we are able to see – even better than in real life – the most subtle changes in facial expressions. However, as it happens, it is Brinchmann's television Nora rather than Garland's cinematic one who is especially expressive in her combination of paralinguistics and mimicry.

In the film and television versions the *camera work* may reveal interesting differences. While Sjöstrand's slight high-angle shot has no indicative value – it is simply a shot from Helmer's optical point of view – that of Garland, showing Nora's face straight-on, is actually manipulating Helmer's optical point of view. In the shot preceding the one transcribed here, this is even more noticeable. There, Garland uses not a slight low-angle shot when showing Helmer's face in close-up, as we might expect, since this would be a shot from Nora's optical point of view, but a marked high-angle shot turning Helmer into 'a child'.

A *property* like the travelling-bag is of little use in the television versions at this point, since the close-ups of the faces most directors would prefer at this climactic moment exclude it from the screen. Instead, the proximity to the door here becomes the visual sign that Nora is about to leave. In Bergman's stage version, by contrast, where close-ups are not possible and where there is no door, the picking up of the bag becomes the signal to the audience that Nora is leaving.

Paralinguistically, there is a considerable difference between the way in which the various Noras enunciate the key line: pertly (Sjöstrand), softly (Garland, Thacker), softly but insistently

(Neuenfels), hesitantly (Brinchmann), or warmly but firmly (Bergman). The tempo also varies a great deal. Thus strategic pauses with Brinchmann and Bergman help to suggest Nora's inner struggle at this point.

The most famous single signifier in *A Doll's House* is the *sound effect* with which the play is concluded:

(The sound of a street door being slammed locked is heard from below.)[6]

The problem with this sound is that it is more informative to the reader than to the spectator. For how can a director make it clear to the audience that the door not only closes but also locks, that no return is possible? Aside from this, every director must ponder precisely when the sound should be heard; how loud it should be; where Helmer, the only person in the room, should be placed at the moment, and so on. Kehlmann, Sjöstrand and Brinchmann abstain from the door slam. Losey shows, rather theatrically, Helmer in a long shot standing stiffly next to the grandfather clock when the slam is heard. Garland, more cinematically, synchronises the door slam with a zoom-in to an extreme close-up of Helmer's face, suggesting that the sound will continue to reverberate in his head. Bergman, at this point devoting himself to aural choreography, places the door slam at the end of Helmer's threefold calling – in crescendo – for Nora, and lets it be followed by his final, desperate whispering of her name.

While four of the directors abstain from *musical effects* at the very end, Saari and Kehlmann resort to a mixture of non-diegetic and diegetic music, whereas Thacker, Garland and Losey conclude their versions with non-diegetic mood music. Garland ends with a sweet, doll-like tune, as from a music-box – the kind of music heard at the beginning of the film. Losey, cutting from a close-up of the fatal letter-box to an exterior long shot of the local church, swept in mist and snow – a striking piece of *editing* – similarly ends with sounds heard in the pre-title sequence of the film.

As my comparison of the nine endings has hopefully demonstrated, the classification scheme may serve as a practical tool when describing, analysing and comparing stage, television and film versions based on one and the same drama text. The scheme can be of use for the tracing of related signifiers as well as for the ordering of the material. By means of the scheme, which allows both for a vertical and a horizontal analysis, correspondences and discrepancies between the drama text and the performance texts can be established with a certain systematic precision, while variables between the performance texts can be notated with a similar exactness.

Is it then legitimate to compare stage and screen performances? Some people would answer this question negatively, arguing that the two media are so different that they can better be studied separately. To my mind, this is throwing the baby out with the bath-water, since it disregards the fact that a number of things, despite media differences, *are* comparable – as the examples presented here verify. Besides, as Esslin points out,

> only by starting from an overview of all the aspects of dramatic performance can we arrive at a clear differentiation of those features that each of the separate media – stage, film and television – can claim as specifically their own, as against the much larger number of aspects they have in common.[7]

George Brandt expresses himself to the same effect when he states that 'in the past it may have been necessary to insist on the difference between the television play and other forms of drama; now it is more useful to point out the similarities'.[8] Accepting this, we are still left with the problem of registration. While screen performances are available in their original form also after the first presentation – in this sense they resemble drama texts – and consequently can be checked by researchers retrospectively, stage performances disintegrate the moment the performance is over. This means that while a video registration of a film and, especially, of a television performance is similar to the intended presentation, a video registration of a stage performance is necessarily rather different to what the director has intended. Since it is usually undertaken without an audience, there is no feed-back for the actors. And since the camera 'concentrates on that area of the stage space where the characters of the given scene are performing', we usually do not see more than part of the stage.[9]

Nevertheless, video registrations form a valuable supplement to notations made in connection with live productions not only because they 'survive' these and, as a consequence, make them accessible to future research but also because they provide a wealth of information simply by being repeatable and by showing details – via medium shots and close-ups – visible only to front row spectators in the theatre. Turning to more practical aspects, we may also note that video registrations of live productions make accurate studies in comparative performance analysis internationally more feasible.

Why do signifiers in one performance text differ from those in another and why do they do it precisely the way they do? Answers to these questions, to be found in relation to the five codes mentioned at the beginning of this chapter, will aim at establishing what is signified by the signifiers. Although this is necessarily a more or less speculative undertaking, it is desirable that it is less so, that is, that the meaning is deduced from careful observation and description of the signifiers. The method applied here is a try-out in this direction. Finding suitable material and appropriate tools are certainly preconditions for meaningful research in the hitherto almost virgin field of comparative performance analysis.

CHAPTER 9

EPILOGUE: IMPACT

'The terrible offstage slamming of that front door which brings down the curtain resounded through more apartments than Torvald Helmer's. No play had ever before contributed so momentously to the social debate, or been so widely and furiously discussed among people who were not normally interested in theatrical or even artistic matters.'[1] The legal consequences of Nora's forgery, had it been brought to court, were discussed at length.[2] While the play was hailed in some quarters, notably among the feminists who tended to see Nora as an apotheosis of the new woman,[3] it was rejected in others. The opposition was especially adamant in countries less emancipated than the Scandinavian ones.[4] In China, for example, productions of *A Doll's House* were forbidden even in the 1920s on the ground that 'the play incited women to leave their homes and their families, and thus ruined the morals of society'. Yet a few years later, after the memorable 1935 Shanghai production, starring Jiang Quing, the future third wife of Mao Tse-tung, the play had a tremendous impact on Chinese theatre. Chinese stage realism simply begins with this performance, effecting a minor cultural revolution.[5]

Three examples of the early English reception of *A Doll's House* may be seen as representative of the general animosity among the (male) critics of the last century:

> It would be a misfortune were such a morbid and unwholesome play to gain the favour of the public. *London Evening Standard*

> Ibsen . . . is too faddy and too obstinately unsympathetic to please English playgoers. *The Sunday Times*

> Cannot be allowed to pass without a word of protest against the
> dreary and sterilizing principle which it seeks to embody.
> *The Observer*[6]

Many of Ibsen's contemporaries objected to Nora's leaving her husband and children. Today most people will probably agree with Nora's decision to leave her husband but find it hard to accept her leaving her young children. In that respect the play is still very provocative.

While most recipients would rest content with imagining what happened after Nora had left her husband and children, some would loudly express their views about what ought to happen. This was done in reviews of the play or of productions of it as well as in articles and books dealing with drama, theatre and, not least, social problems, notably those pertaining to man–woman relations. It is beyond the range of this book to discuss the socio-political repercussions of *A Doll's House*, its importance for the women's liberation movement, and so on. It is also outside its scope to trace its influence on writers all over the world, a gigantic task that could only be undertaken as a team project. Instead, we shall examine the play's impact on five outstanding dramatists and one prominent filmmaker. How did Ibsen's play influence works composed in the same or in a related medium?

Before we do this we must pay passing attention to a special category: the plays written in direct and explicit response to Ibsen's drama.

Few plays, if any, have resulted in so many sequels and parodies as *A Doll's House*. Already in 1881 the Norwegian M.J. Bugge published his *How Nora Returned Home Again: An Epilogue.* In the same year the New Theatre in Helsinki presented F. Wahlberg's *The Impossible Possible.*

In Britain, a parody of Ibsen's drama actually preceded the play itself in the theatre. On 3 March 1884 an adaptation by Henry Arthur Jones and Henry Herman, entitled *Breaking a Butterfly*, premièred at the Prince's Theatre in London. Harley Granville-Barker gives a vivid description of the play:

The scene is laid in some English country town. Nora becomes
Flora, and to her husband, rather terribly, Flossie. He is Humphrey
Goddard and we find him gifted with a mother (quite unnecessarily)
and a sister (wanted for the piano playing *vice* Mrs Linden, who
disappears). Torvald-Humphrey behaves like the paste-board hero
of Nora's doll's house dream; he *does* strike his chest and say 'I am the
guilty one'. And Flora-Nora cries that she is a poor weak foolish girl,
'. . . no wife for a man like you. You are a thousand times too good
for me', and never wakes up and walks out of her doll's house at all.[7]

Breaking a Butterfly exemplifies one way of disarming Ibsen's shock-
ing play, by ridiculing it and by applying the alternative conciliatory
ending.

Six years later Walter Besant's *The Doll's House – and After* warns
against the dangerous consequences of Nora's exit.[8] Twenty years
have passed. Torvald and Ivar are alcoholics, Bob turns a forgerer
and Emma commits suicide. In the same year, 1890, Ednah D.
Cheney issued her *Nora's Return. A Sequel to 'The Doll's House of
Henrik Ibsen'* in Boston. A year later Israel Zangwill and Eleanor
Marx, daughter of Karl, published their '*A Doll's House* Repaired' in
Time. In this sequel Nora returns to Helmer

in a mood of great contrition and despair, and submits to his plans to
keep their marriage going on a platonic basis – just for appearance's
sake. The story ends not with Nora slamming the front door on
Helmer, but with Helmer slamming the bedroom door on Nora.[9]

In 1903, finally, Marie Itzerott's *Nora or Above Our Strength*
appeared in Strassburg.

The revived interest in *A Doll's House* in the late 1960s and early
1970s was noticeable also in the dramatised sequels and/or alterna-
tives that appeared in this period. A sequel by the Danish playwright
Ernst Bruun Olsen was published in 1969 in German translation by
Udo Birckholz under the title *Where did Nora go? Folk Comedy in
Three Acts* and was performed in Saarbrücken four years later. Bruun

Olsen's Nora characteristically joins the workers, representatives of another suppressed group, to fight bourgeois class society.[10]

The Nora of Clare Booth Luce's '*A Doll's House*, 1970', later called *Slam the Door Softly*,[11] lives in a comfortable middle-class 'suburb of New York'. She is

> liberated by the pill from inevitable motherhood, liberated intel-
> lectually by her education, and liberated from culturally conditioned
> self-deprecation by feminist writers from de Beauvoir to Mary
> Ellman and Kate Millett – [and] closes the door, very gently, on a
> much loved husband for whom the 'miracle' has not yet happened.[12]

Esther Vilar's Nora, in *Helmer or A Doll's House: Variations on a Theme by Henrik Ibsen* from 1979, returns to her husband only to treat *him* as a doll.[13]

As with Bruun Olsen, Elfriede Jelinek's Nora – in *What Happened after Nora Had Left her Husband or Pillars of Societies*, 1977–8 – starts out as a factory worker. But very soon she returns to a second doll's existence, at the side of a capitalist magnate. In her various roles, Jelinek's Nora shows herself to be a puppet pulled by capitalist strings.[14]

Finally, Tormod Skagestad's sequel *Nora Helmer*,[15] written in New Norwegian, opens with Nora's return – the day after she has left! She has rapidly reached the conclusion that she cannot manage alone, since she has not learned anything. Prepared to stay in Helmer's house, she insists, however, that they remain separated. Helmer, attempting to win Nora back, spoils her with expensive presents, paid for with money from the bank. When Krogstad, now assistant manager of the bank, discovers his crime, he once more gets the upper hand over the Helmers. While the men wish to cover the thing up, Nora insists on telling the truth in a *roman à clef* she is about to publish. At the end of the play it is clear that Helmer must leave Nora – for prison. By deliberately sticking closely to Ibsen's text, Skagestad manages to create a number of significant echo effects and ironical reversals in his three-act sequel.

Ever since it was published, Ibsen's *Doll's House* has generally been seen as the most forceful plea in world literature for equality between the sexes. Men and women, husbands and wives, fathers and mothers – this is its credo – are all in the first place 'human beings'. Self-realisation is its emancipatory key word. Like Ibsen, Strindberg pleaded for a number of reforms that would make women socially more equal to men. But unlike him, he believed that sexual differences are fundamental and that equality must therefore be combined with a gender-determined division of labour.

Strindberg had won the reputation of being the leading radical writer in Sweden. But he could not go along with the emancipatory ideas of 'the Nora man', as he contemptuously called Ibsen. Three years after the publication of *A Doll's House* Strindberg brought out his three-act drama *Sir Bengt's Wife*, which can be seen as a direct answer to Ibsen's play. As Ulf Boëthius in particular has demonstrated,[16] there are striking similarities between the two plays. Both deal with marriages in which the husband regards his wife as a delicate bird which he must protect from harsh reality. And both husbands fail to live up to the expectations of their wives, who want to get divorced from them.

Strindberg no doubt deliberately patterned his play on Ibsen's to bring his own very different views on the woman question into greater relief. For in *Sir Bengt's Wife* it is not the wife but the husband who silently sacrifices himself to save his partner. While Sir Bengt's altruism echoes Nora's, his wife Margit, like Helmer, is an egoistic aesthete. Nora's discovery that she is not in the first place 'wife and mother', as her husband would have it, but 'first and foremost a human being', is parodied by Strindberg in Margit's: 'My life before God is worth more than that of this child, for I am a human being, and the child isn't that as yet.' At the end of the play Margit, cleansed from her selfishness, agrees to stay with her husband. In opposition to Ibsen, who in his play stresses the need for the husband to change, Strindberg in *Sir Bengt's Wife* advocates a change on the part of the wife.

Both Ibsen and Strindberg were highly sceptical of the society in which they lived, but while Ibsen was so primarily because it was a male society, in which women were suppressed, Strindberg opposed society because it was too removed from nature. In a wider, Darwinian-Rousseauan sense, he argued in the preface to his collection of short stories *Getting Married* (1884) that both men and women are victims of the repressive mechanisms of modern society. To Strindberg the difference between 'natural' and 'cultural' man was of fundamental importance. Rather than imitate the cultural males, who were on the wrong track, women should return to their natural, biological roles of being mothers in the first place.

One of the stories in *Getting Married*, entitled 'A Doll's House', deals with the marriage between Captain Pall and Gurli. While he is at sea, a religious spinster, Ottilia, indoctrinates Gurli with emancipatory ideas derived from Ibsen's play. Identifying herself with the suppressed Nora, Gurli sends her husband a copy of the play. He reads it and writes her a letter in which he repeats many of the criticisms that Strindberg had delivered in the preface to the book. When Pall, back home, calculatingly begins to flirt with Ottilia, Gurli becomes jealous and sends her woman friend packing. And the story ends with husband and wife happily reunited in what he calls 'a genuine doll's house'.

Although both Strindberg and Pall reveal a prejudiced misunderstanding of *A Doll's House*, their basic idea that Ibsen has stacked the cards against the man in favour of the woman is a view that makes more sense now than when it was first articulated, simply because woman's social position has improved a great deal since Ibsen wrote his play.

This is how Pall, in his letter to his wife, sketches the end of *A Doll's House* the way Ibsen ought to have written it. Says Helmer: 'You, my little Nora, were badly brought up, I, old fool that I am, hadn't learnt any better. Pity us both! Throw rotten eggs at our educators but don't just hit me on the head. Although I am a man, I am as innocent as you are!' Apparently remarking on Ibsen's play, Pall is obliquely commenting on his own marriage. His idea of mutual and equal guilt provides a basis for a new relationship between husband and wife. Via Pall Strindberg indicates a possible happy ending of *A Doll's House*, very different from the ones Ibsen chose to write.

Once more, in his comedy *Marauders* (1886), Strindberg created a situation similar to the one in *A Doll's House*, only to demonstrate the mental superiority of the husband as compared to his wife.[17] The title refers to the pseudo-Darwinian idea that woman, after thousands of years of male development, mistakenly believes that she has the right to come marauding into his territory. While Strindberg could certainly find some sympathy among men for such statements, it is likely that he indirectly only helped to make others sympathise with 'the Nora man'.

George Bernard Shaw's interest in *A Doll's House*, best known from his comments on the play in *The Quintessence of Ibsenism* (1891), is presumably the major reason for a rather slanted view of Ibsen's play in Britain and America. Deeply concerned with social questions, Shaw was at first mainly interested in Ibsen's play as the work that 'gave Victorian domestic morality its death-blow'. Much later, in a chapter added to his *Quintessence* in 1913, he stressed the novelty of the play structure.[18] 'Formerly', Shaw states,

> you had in what was called a well made play an exposition in the first act, a situation in the second, and unravelling in the third. Now you have exposition, situation and discussion; . . . The discussion conquered Europe in Ibsen's *Doll's House*; and now the serious playwright recognizes in the discussion not only the main test of his highest powers, but also the real centre of his play's interest. . . . And it was by this new technical feature: this addition of a new movement, as musicians would say, to the dramatic form, that *A Doll's House* conquered Europe and founded a new school of dramatic art.[19]

Shaw then goes on to criticise Ibsen for *ending* his play with the discussion. A better way, he says, is either 'to begin with discussion and end with action' – as he himself had done in some of his plays – or let the discussion interpenetrate 'the action from beginning to end'. Rather than being convincing arguments, these statements indicate above all Shaw's ambition to improve on Ibsen's invention. Few would claim that he succeeded in this ambition.

The same tendency to pick up ideas from Ibsen and refashion them can be seen in some of Shaw's plays. By reversing the situation in *A Doll's House* in his three-act play *Candida* (1894), Shaw tried to demonstrate that, as he put it, 'in the real typical doll's house it is the man who is the doll'.[20] Candida treats her husband Morell as a child. Like Helmer, Morell

> does find out at the end of the play what he owes to his wife, and we discover in each case that the apparently strong, protective man is in reality weaker than his wife. These connections would not likely have escaped the first London audience seeing *Candida* in 1900 with Janet Achurch, the original Nora five years before Shaw's play was written, as Candida – especially members of the audience who knew that the part of Candida was written for her.[21]

The implicit erotic triangle Helmer–Nora–Rank in *Candida* has its counterpart in Morell–Candida–Marchbanks. But in Shaw's play it is the platonic lover, not the wife, who leaves for the darkness outside. Impressed as he was with the discussion in *A Doll's House*, Shaw included a discussion in *Candida*, and as in Ibsen's play, it begins with an invitation to sit down and talk.

Like Nora, Liza Doolittle in *Pygmalion* (1912), picked up from the street, undergoes a remarkable transformation in the course of the play. Humiliated by her upper-class benefactor, Liza

> is a doll in Henry Higgins's doll house. Shaw himself hints at the resemblance when he has Mrs Higgins accuse her son and Pickering of being 'a pretty pair of babies, playing with your live doll'. Like Nora . . . she becomes self-reliant. Like Nora . . . she leaves the doll house, an independent human being.[22]

In 1903 Shaw's countryman John Millington Synge made his debut

with the one-acter *The Shadow of the Glen*. Although Synge explicitly opposed the 'joyless' Norwegian dramatist, statements of this
kind may well have been made to disguise Ibsen's impact. Despite
the great dissimilarity between the environment in *The Shadow of
the Glen* and *A Doll's House*, there is

> more than one connecting link between Synge's Nora and her
> Norwegian namesake . . . Both plays introduce us to an ill-assorted
> couple whose union is spoilt by a bullying husband who does not
> allow his wife any kind of private life. Furthermore . . . in either
> drama the final exposure of the heroine is followed by a great
> *scène à faire*, ending up with the woman banging the door on her
> husband. . . . Both dramas close with a question-mark.[23]

Shaw served as an important link between Ibsen and America's foremost dramatist, Eugene O'Neill. Already at the age of seventeen,
O'Neill 'was wildly excited about Shaw's *Quintessence of Ibsenism*. It
was his favorite reading.'[24] In October 1906 Alla Nazimova had put
on a repertory of Ibsen: *A Doll's House, Hedda Gabler, The Master
Builder*. O'Neill went to see them all 'and he talked Ibsen all that
year'.[25]

As one might expect, the influence of *A Doll's House* is particularly
obvious in O'Neill's earliest plays. Mrs Baldwin, the unfaithful wife
in *Recklessness* (1913), a one-act melodrama, characterises her husband in words that could have been Nora's after the awakening:

> He has looked upon me as a plaything, the slave of his pleasure, a
> pretty toy to be exhibited that others might envy him his ownership.
> But he's given me everything I've ever asked for without a word –
> more than I ever asked for. He hasn't ever known what the word
> 'husband' ought to mean but he's been a very considerate 'owner'.[26]

Just as the guilt is not solely Helmer's but also Nora's father's, who, as
she says, 'played with me as I played with dolls', so Baldwin can partly refute his wife's criticism: 'If I have regarded you as a plaything I
was only accepting the valuation your parents set upon you when
they sold you.'[27]

Servitude (1914), O'Neill's first full-length play, was 'probably inspired by *A Doll's House*'; but it is more doubtful whether its play-wright-protagonist, David Roylston, whose play, *Sacrifice*, might in fact have been entitled *A Doll's House*, was 'intended to represent Ibsen'.[28] Mrs Frazer, the wife of a broker, tells Roylston:

> I had been to see your play 'Sacrifice' . . . for the tenth time. It
> seemed to breathe a message to me over the footlights. You
> remember when Mrs Harding in the play leaves her husband with
> the words: 'I have awakened!'? . . . I felt that I, too, had awakened.[29]

By following the example of Mrs Harding, Mrs Frazer, too, momen-tarily becomes another Nora:

> I was in love with an ideal – the ideal of self-realization, of the duty
> of the individual to assert its supremacy and demand the freedom
> necessary for its development. . . . I saw I could never hope to grow
> in the stifling environment of married life – so I broke away.[30]

Roylston shares her ideal – until the end of the play. Then both of them convert. She returns to her husband. And he expounds his newly gained philosophy of 'sacrifice' and 'servitude', an awakened Helmer, as it were. The conclusion is thus totally different from that of *A Doll's House*, so much so that O'Neill's play might easily be taken to be a rejoinder to Nora's plea for self-realisation, a sequel to Ibsen's drama showing how Nora repents and stays at home. Yet, since O'Neill's Helmer does change, we are more correct in seeing Roylston's home as a doll's house, which through his repentance, ceases to be just that.

Among Ibsen's own countrymen, the impact of *A Doll's House* has been most obvious on Helge Krog, next to Nordahl Grieg the lead-ing Norwegian playwright of the 1930s. Krog's *Breakup* (1936) deals with the need to liberate oneself from the constraints of con-ventional life to create a basis for spiritual growth and fulfilment. Sharing the retrospective technique, the tightly knit plot and the basic theme with Ibsen's drama, *Breakup* has actually been called 'an updated version of *A Doll's House*: 'Even the ending – with the heroine, Vibeke, leaving her lover and her husband (whom she now, for the first time, sees unmasked) – is the same, though perhaps without the shock effect of Nora's exit in 1879.'[31]

Of special interest in our context is Ingmar Bergman's affinity to Ibsen's play. His familiarity with it goes back at least to the late 1940s, when Hollywood producer David O. Selznick wanted him to do a screen version of *A Doll's House*. The film was to be directed by Alf Sjöberg, who a few years earlier had directed a film based on Bergman's first screenplay. But, Bergman later said, 'Sjöberg had too many ideas and I had too few', and no film materialised.[32]

That Ibsen's play nevertheless lingered on in Bergman's mind appears from the many similarities to it that can be found in his films. Already in *Summer with Monika* (1952) we come across a wife, Monika, who walks out on her husband, Harry. At the end we see him, left alone, embracing their little daughter. Moreover, like Nora, Monika recognises a parallel between her father's and her husband's treatment of her.

Anne Egerman in *Smiles of a Summer Night* (1955) is a 'child bride', married to a prominent, middle-aged lawyer. Like Nora she feels superfluous in her own home, squeezed between the working men – her husband and his son – and the working women, the servants. Nora's rehearsing for the fancy-dress ball has its counterpart in Anne's dressing up for the theatre:

> Oh, Fredrik! How nice. Are we going to the theater tonight? What am I going to wear? How did you find time? How wonderful! What shall I wear? Just think, you've found time to go to the theater with your little Anne.[33]

This is very much Ibsen's lark enthusiastically looking forward to something 'wonderful', not a real-life event but an illusory imitation of life, a theatre performance.

In *Cries and Whispers* (1973) one of the three sisters, Maria, is depicted as a child wife brought up by a single parent, in this case a mother. (Both parts are played by Liv Ullmann.) In one sequence we see her, thumb in mouth, very much like a doll, in her former girl's room, looking at her old doll's house. In another one, she is seen together with her little daughter, who is carrying a doll. The suggestion is that mother, daughter and granddaughter are all part of the same 'doll' tradition, a tradition that Maria's daughter is obviously doomed to continue. Unlike Nora, Maria never matures. Having been quite close to her sister Karin for a moment, she reverts at the end of the film to her doll's role.

With the extremely successful television series *Scenes from a Marriage* (1973) Bergman created a doll's house relationship for our time. Johan and Marianne are in many respects Helmer and Nora a century later. Toward the end of the series, Marianne remarks: 'Superficially, the relationship between men and women has changed. But in reality it's the same as a hundred years ago.' One of the 'superficial' changes is that Marianne, unlike Nora, has a profession. Without one she would not be a representative Swedish wife of the 1970s. But the independence is tempered by the fact that Marianne, who is a lawyer, has chosen the same profession as her father. Johan is 'an associate professor at the Psychotechnical Institute'. They are both 'inheritors of a faith in fixed norms and material security. They have never found their bourgeois way of life oppressive or false.'[34]

Not surprisingly, their living-room is very similar to that of the Helmers. When we first see them, they are sitting together on a sofa that is

round and curved and nineteenth century and upholstered in green; it has friendly arms, soft cushions, and carved legs; it is a monstrosity of cosiness. A pretty paraffin lamp can be glimpsed on a table. The background consists of a massive bookcase.[35]

This living-room, like that of the Helmers, is an aesthetic and cosy bourgeois façade, advertising that the people inhabiting it are cultivated and happily married. Its old-fashioned furniture suggests an inherited conservative taste.

If Nora has been treated as a doll by her father, Johan and Marianne have been brought up in the same way by their mothers. 'For my sisters and me', Marianne complains, 'our entire upbringing was aimed at our being *agreeable*.' As a result, she finds that she has been much too considerate towards her husband and that this 'consideration killed off love'.

Early in the series Johan and Marianne characteristically discuss *A Doll's House*, which they have just seen in the theatre. Ironically, their divergent opinions with regard to woman's social and conjugal position echo those of Ibsen's couple – as if little has changed in man–woman relations in the past hundred years. Sharing Strindberg's view in the woman question, Johan declares:

> What do women want in parliament or in the government? It would only force them to share a responsibility. They would lose their comfortable role of opposition. They would have to get rid of their pet vices: bringing up children and letting themselves be supported and oppressed.[36]

However, unlike Helmer's male chauvinist view, Johan's anti-feminism seems above all determined by a need to project his (male) guilt feelings on the opposite sex; he still at this point keeps the fact that he has a mistress hidden from his wife.

Like Ibsen, Bergman counters his primary couple with a secondary one, Peter and Katarina. But whereas Ibsen's secondary couple is included to demonstrate how they move in a direction contrary to that of the primary one, Bergman's couple is included to dramatise Johan's and Marianne's repressed aggressiveness toward one another.

More reminiscent of Mrs Linde than Katarina is another catalyst: Mrs Jacobi. Mrs Jacobi has come to see Marianne, her lawyer, about her divorce. After a long marriage, she has decided to leave her husband. It is only because of their three children that she has not done so long ago. Her husband has always been kind and faithful to her but, she keeps repeating, 'there is no love in the marriage' – and there never has been.

Her situation is obviously similar to Mrs Linde's and, obliquely, to Nora's. Like Mrs Linde, Mrs Jacobi has chosen to stay with her husband until the children have grown up and become independent. Just as Mrs Linde is a foil for Nora, so Mrs Jacobi is a foil for Marianne. In both cases the 'visitors' undermine the protagonist's illusory feelings of conjugal happiness and serve to initiate the process of self-examination.

Although Nora has been evaluated rather differently, most people would certainly be more sympathetic to her than to Helmer. As we have seen, this constitutes a problem when presenting the play today. Most directors nowadays would prefer to see not only Nora but also Helmer as a victim of rigid social norms. Long before Bergman staged *A Doll's House* along these lines, he had, in *Scenes from a Marriage*, created a rather balanced situation, seeing both husband and wife as immature children pulled by social and biological strings, notably navel strings. While Ibsen has the wife leave husband and children to find her own identity, Bergman has the husband leave wife and children for another woman. This is a very recognisable event in the divorce era. But it lacks the ideological explosiveness of Nora's decision.

Bergman's ending is even more open than Ibsen's. While we may doubt that Nora will ever return to her husband, we wonder whether Johan and Marianne, each of them remarried, will stay with their new partners or divorce them, reunite and start anew. If Bergman's ending seems slightly more optimistic, it is because we sense that Johan and Marianne have *both* changed, a process made possible by the much longer time span of the series as compared to the play.

In its relation to *A Doll's House*, *Scenes from a Marriage* takes a unique position. Unlike most sequels – a misnomer in this case – it is a work of art in its own right. Although it lacks the provocative power of Ibsen's play, it is as painfully recognisable in its depiction of man–woman relations. No other work showing such an affinity to *A Doll's House* has had such an impact on so many people. Especially in affluent societies with a high divorce rate, to millions of married couples *Scenes from a Marriage* has seemed like a mirror of their own situation, in many families presumably initiating a process of self-examination similar to the one taking place in the series. Being the work of an author-cum-director, much of what we find in the TV series has spilt over into Bergman's two stage productions of *A Doll's House*, his stage version of *Scenes from a Marriage* (1981) serving as an intermediate link. The series is a key to an understanding of these productions.

Bergman was to return to the doll theme in *Autumn Sonata* (1978), set in Norway. Nora's problematic upbringing and conjugal relationship here has its counterpart in Eva's situation. Eva, whose mother is a famous concert pianist, always on tour, has virtually been brought up by her father. Like Nora, she has married a man who is an obvious substitute for her beloved father. And just as Nora at the end of Ibsen's play is concerned with her own lack of identity, so Eva in the beginning of Bergman's film states: 'The biggest obstacle [to genuine living] is that I don't know who I am.'[37] The film describes how mother and daughter meet again after seven years. And how the daughter, who has always adored her distant mother, in the middle of the night at long last rids herself of all her repressions and launches a terrible attack on her, opening with the following Ibsenite accusation: 'To you I was a doll that you played with when you had time. If I was sick or naughty, you handed me over to the nanny or to Father.'[38]

It takes no sharp eye to see that the mother–daughter relationship in *Autumn Sonata* is akin not only to that between Nora and her father but also to that between Nora and Helmer. It is also obvious that Eva's nocturnal outburst has its predecessor in Nora's decision, in the middle of the night, to sit down and talk seriously with her husband for the first time after eight years of marriage. But while Nora's criticism of Helmer is tempered by her criticism of herself,

Eva one-sidedly blames her mother for everything that has gone wrong.

As we have seen, Shaw claimed that *A Doll's House* 'conquered Europe and founded a new school of dramatic art'. Both statements are valid. The play has in fact by now conquered the world, and it has done so thanks to what Shaw termed 'the discussion', the part for which, according to Ibsen himself, the whole play was written. However, what Shaw disregards is that it is the combination of the dicussion and Nora's departure that does the trick. Nora not only talks, she also acts. At the end of the play Nora questions what to most people was an axiomatic social institution: marriage. She then, logically, divorces her husband – to face a future on her own. What will it be like? By providing the play with an open ending, Ibsen forced the recipients to take a stand in a matter that must have concerned many of them directly.

Strindberg in 1887 claimed that 'the theatre is a weapon'.[39] Eight years earlier Ibsen had proved it – with *A Doll's House*. And he still does whenever the play is imaginatively performed. As Shaw prophesied in 1913: 'There comes a time . . . when the parable of the doll's house is more to our purpose than the parable of the prodigal son.'[40]

SEQUENCE SCHEME OF 'ET DUKKEHJEM/ A DOLL'S HOUSE'

Abbreviation of characters (in order of appearance)

 M = Maid (Helene)
 N = Nora
 P = Porter
 H = Helmer
ML = Mrs Linde
 K = Krogstad
 R = Rank
Ch = The Helmers' three children
Nu = Nurse (Anne-Marie)
 [] = Speaking character invisible
  * = Key sequences

Page/line references are to Henrik Ibsen, *Samlede Verker: Hundreårsutgave*, VIII, Oslo: Gyldendal, 1933, and to Henrik Ibsen, *Plays: Two* (tr. Michael Meyer), London: Methuen, 1982

Act I

Seq	On stage							S. V.	Meyer
1								273/13	23/14
2	M							273/13	23/14
3	M	N						273/13	23/15
4	M	N	P					273/16	23/18
5		N	P					273/19	23/22
6		N						273/23	23/26
7		N	[H]					273/28	24/3
*8		N	H					274/4	24/12
9	M	N	H					278/31	28/26
10	M	N		ML				279/3	28/31
*11		N		ML				279/5	28/33
12	M	N		ML				290/6	38/6
13		N		ML	K			290/12	38/10
14		N		ML				290/23	38/20
15		N		ML	R			291/8	39/3
16		N	H	ML	R			293/34	41/15
17		N	H	ML	R	Ch	Nu	295/22	42/33
18		N				Ch	Nu	295/30	43/4
19		N				Ch		296/12	43/20
20		N			K	Ch		296/26	44/2
*21		N			K			297/6	44/18
22								304/4	50/16
23		N				Ch		304/9	50/21
24		N						304/19	50/31
25	M	N						304/24	51/3
26		N						304/29	51/8
*27		N	H					305/1	51/13
28		N						308/18	54/19
29		N					Nu	308/20	54/21
30		N						308/26–28	54/26–28

Act II

Seq	On stage						S. V.	Meyer
31		N					309/5	55/4
32		N				Nu	309/14	55/14
33		N					310/33	55/26
*34		N		ML			311/6	56/33
35		N	H				314/27	60/10
36	M	N	H				318/2	63/6
37		N	H				318/8	63/11
38		N					319/10	64/8
*39		N			R		319/16	64/15
40	M	N			R		324/15	68/25
41		N			R		324/16	68/26
42	M	N			R		325/16	69/29
43	M	N					326/9	70/9
44		N					326/21	70/18
45	M	N			K		326/24	70/20
*46		N			K		326/25	70/22
47		N					330/13	73/27
48		N		ML			330/23	74/3
49		N	[H]	ML			332/4	75/12
50		N	[H]				332/22	75/31
51		N	H				332/25	75/33
*52		N	H		R		332/28	76/3
53		N	H	ML	R		334/18	77/25
54	M	N	H	ML	R		335/12	78/19
55		N		ML			335/16	78/22
56		N		ML			335/30	78/35
57		N					336/8	79/12
58		N	H				336/12–14	79/16–18

	On stage					S. V.	Meyer
59				ML		337/6	80/5
*60				ML	K	337/14	80/15
61				ML		342/3	84/16
62		N	H	ML		342/9	84/25
63		N		ML		343/25	86/3
64		N	H	ML		344/3	86/13
65		N	H			344/29	87/3
66		N	H		[R]	346/23	88/26
*67		N	H		R	346/26	88/28
68		N	H			349/7	90/28
69		N				351/4	92/21
*70		N	H			351/12	92/29
71	M	N	H			353/23	94/30
72		N	H			353/25	94/32
73		[N]	H			355/7	96/6
*74		N	H			356/3	96/32
75			H			363/5	103/4
76		N	H			363/6	103/6
77			H			364/29–32	104/20–23

SELECT LIST OF PRODUCTIONS

ABBREVIATIONS

Tr.   = translation
Adapt. = adaptation
Dir.   = direction
Sc.   = scenography
N   = Nora
H   = Helmer

STAGE

1879   21 Dec. *Et Dukkehjem*, Royal Theatre, Copenhagen. Dir.
           H.P. Holst. N Betty Hennings, H Emil Poulsen.

1880   8 Jan. *Ett dockhem*, Royal Dramatic Theatre, Stockholm.
           N Anna Lisa Hwasser, H Gustav Fredrikson.

1880   20 Jan. Christiania Theatre. N Johanne Juell, H Arnoldus
           Reimers.

1880   28 Feb. Suomalainen Theatre, Helsinki. N Ida Ålberg.

1880   3 Mar. *Nora oder Ein Puppenheim*, Residenztheater,
           Munich. Dir. Ernst von Possart. N Marie Ramlo-Conrad.

1880   22 Nov. Residenztheater, Berlin. N Hedwig Niemann-Raabe.

1881   8 Sept. Stadttheater, Vienna. Dir. Heinrich Laube.

1881   Nov. Polish Theatre, St Petersburg. N Helena Modjeska.

1882   10 Mar. Imperial Theatre, Warsaw. N Helena Modjeska.

1882   2 Jun. *The Child Wife*. Adapt. Grand Opera House,
           Milwaukee. Tr. William Moorse Lawrence. Eva [N]
           Minerva Guernsey, H Robert Harman.

1883   25 Jan. St Petersburg. N Gabriela Zapolska.

7 Dec. *Thora*. Macauley's Theatre, Louisville, Kentucky. N Helena Modjeska.

1884   8 Feb. Alexandrinsky Theatre, St Petersburg. N Maria Savina.

1884   3 Mar. *Breaking a Butterfly*. Adapt. Prince's Theatre, London.

1887   Oct. Stadttheater, Cologne. N Mrs Milan-Doré.

1888   Carl-Theater, Vienna. N Friederikke Gossmann.

1888   May. German Theatre, Prague. N Johanna Buska.

1888   25 Nov. Lessing Theater, Berlin. N Lilli Petri.

1889   3 Mar. Théâtre du Parc, Brussels. Dir. Léon Vanderkindere.

1889   29 Mar. *Een poppenhuis*, Grand Théâtre, Amsterdam. Dir. Louis Moor. N Aleida Roelofsen, H Jan Malherbe.

1889   7 Jun. Novelty Theatre, London. Tr. William Archer. N Janet Achurch, H Herbert Waring.

1889   21 Dec. *A Doll's Home*. Palmer's Theatre, New York. N Beatrice Cameron.

1890   26 Sept. Christiania Theatre. N Johanne Dybwad.

1891   9 Feb. *Casa di Bambola*. Teatro di Filodrammatici, Milan. Tr. Luigi Capauana. N Eleonora Duse.

1893   11 Mar. Royalty Theatre, London. N Janet Achurch.

1893   9 Jun. Lyric Theatre, London. N Eleonora Duse.

1894   15 Feb. Empire Theatre, New York. N Minnie Maddern Fiske.

1894   20 Apr. *Maison de poupée*, Théâtre du Vaudeville, Paris. Dir. Herman Bang. N Gabrielle Réjane.

1894   Sept. Deutsches Theater, Berlin. Dir. Otto Brahm. N Agnes Sorma.

1895   18 Sept. Suvorin Theatre, St Petersburg. N Lydia Yavorska.

1897   12 Apr. Irving Place Theatre, New York. N Agnes Sorma.

1897   10 May. Globe Theatre, London. N Janet Achurch, H Courtenay Thorpe.

1899   20 Mar. Gärtner Theater, Munich. N Agnes Sorma.

1899   28 Sept. Schiller Theater, Berlin. N Gertrud Eysoldt.

1904   17 Sept. St Petersburg. N Vera Kommisarjevskaya.

1905   2 May. New Lycaeum Theatre, New York. N Ethel Barrymore.

1906   29 Nov. National Theatre, Christiania. Dir. Olaf Hansson.
       N Johanne Dybwad, H Halfdan Christensen.
1906   Berlin. Dir. Otto Brahm. N Irene Triesch.
1906   18 Dec. Kommisarjevskaya Theatre, St Petersburg. Dir.
       Vsevolod Meyerhold. N Vera Kommisarjevskaya.
1907   14 Jan. Princess Theatre, New York. N Alla Nazimova.
1908   Mar. Daly's Theatre, New York. N Vera Kommisarjevskaya.
1911   14 Feb. Royalty Theatre, London. N Lydia Yavorska.
1911   22 Apr. Kingsway Theatre, London. N Janet Achurch.
1917   23 Nov. Kammerspiele, Berlin. Dir. Max Reinhardt.
       N Lucie Höflich.
1918   29 Apr. Plymouth Theatre, New York. Dir. Arthur
       Hopkins. N Alla Nazimova, H Lionel Atwill.
1920   6 Aug. Lenin Theatre, Novorossisk. Dir. Vsevolod
       Meyerhold.
1922   Central Theatre, Oslo. N Gyda Christensen, H Theodor
       Berge.
1923   Deutsches Theater, Berlin. N Käthe Dorsch.
1925   Royal Dramatic Theatre, Stockholm. N Harriet Bosse,
       H Sven Bergwall.
1925   20 Nov. Playhouse Theatre, London. N Madge Titheradge,
       H Milton Rosmer.
1928   20 Mar. Kingsway Theatre, London. N Gillian Scaife,
       H Gerard Neville.
1930   14 Apr. Criterion Theatre, London. N Gwen Ffrangcon-
       Davies, H Henry Oscar.
1930   Schillertheater, Berlin. Dir. Jürgen Fehling. N Lucie
       Mannheim, H Hans Leibelt.
1934   4 Mar. Arts Theatre, London. N Lydia Lopokova, H Walter
       Hudd.
1935   Ye yu ju ren xie hui, Shanghai. N Jiang Quing.
1936   2 Mar. Criterion Theatre, London. Dir. Leon M. Lion.
       N Lydia Lopokova, H Geoffrey Edwards.
1936   Comedy Theatre, Stockholm. Dir. Ernst Eklund. N Alice
       Eklund, H Björn Berglund.

1936 National Theatre, Oslo. Dr. Halfdan Christensen. Sc. Rahe
Raheny. N Tore Segelcke, H Lasse Segelcke.

1937 27 Dec. Morosco Theatre, New York. Tr. and adapt.
Thornton Wilder. Dir. Jed Harris. N Ruth Gordon,
H Dennis King.

1939 3 Feb. *Nora.* Duke of York's Theatre, London. Dir. Marius
Goring. N Lucie Mannheim, H Austin Trevor.

1939 Renaissance-Theater, Berlin. Dir. Alfred Bernau. N Hilde
Hildebrandt, H Hansjoachim Büttner.

1943 Deutsches Theater, Berlin. Dir. Heinz Hilpert. N Hilde
Krahl, H Hans Brausewetter.

1945 11 July. Arts Theatre, London. N Jenny Laird, H Cyril
Luckham.

1946 17 Jan. Winter Garden Theatre, London. N Angela
Baddeley, H John Stuart.

1952 Comédie Caumartin, Paris. Dir. Jean Mercure. N Danielle
Delorme, H Pierre Asso.

1953 8 Sept. Lyric Theatre, Hammersmith. Dir. Peter Ashmore.
Sc. Reece Pemberton. N Mai Zetterling, H Mogens Wieth.

1953 Schlossparktheater, Berlin. Dir. Boleslaw Barlog. N Käthe
Braun, H Wilhelm Borchert.

1955 Royal Theatre, Copenhagen. Dir. Gerda Ring. N Ingeborg
Brams, H Ebbe Rode.

1955 Swedish National Theatre Centre, Västerås. Dir. Per-Axel
Branner. N Gunn Wållgren.

1956 New Theatre, Oslo. Dir. Claes Gill. N Lillebil Ibsen.

1956 Artistic Youth Theatre of China, Beijing. Dir. Wu Xue.
Artistic adviser Gerda Ring. N Chi Shu-ping.

1958 Spisská Nová Ves Theatre, Czechoslovakia. Dir. Milan
Bobula.N Brigita Bobulová, H Ján Misura.

1962 Royal Dramatic Theatre, Stockholm. Tr. Herbert
Grevenius. Dir. Per-Axel Branner. Sc. Yngve Larson.
N Gunn Wållgren, H Olof Widgren.

1966 27 Jan. Norwegian Theatre, Oslo. Tr. and dir. Tormod

Skagestad. Sc. Arne Walentin. N Monna Tandberg, H Per Theodor Haugen.

1967 22 Feb. Bremer Theater, Kammerspiele. Tr. Richard Linder. Dir. Peter Zadek, Sc. Guy Sheppard. N Edith Clever, H Hans Peter Hallwachs.

1971 Akademietheater, Vienna. Dir. Gerhard Hering. N Elisabeth Orth, H Walter Reyer.

1972 Württemberg Theatre, Stuttgart. Tr. Georg Schulte-Frohlinde. Dir. Hans Neuenfels. Sc. Klaus Gelhaar. N Elisabeth Trissenaar, H Peter Roggisch.

1972 7 Oct. Royal Dramatic Theatre, Stockholm. Tr. Ernst Schönaich. Dir. Frank Sundström. Sc. Sture Pyk. N Bibi Andersson, H Bengt Virdestam.

1972 1 Nov. Greenwich Theatre, London. N Susan Hampshire.

1973 20 Feb. Criterion Theatre, London. Dir. Patrick Garland. N Claire Bloom, Colin Blakeley.

1974 24 Jan. Norwegian Theatre, Oslo. Tr. Tormod Skagestad. Dir. Pål Skjønsberg and Elisabeth Bang. Sc. Arne Walentin. N Liv Ullmann, H Odd Furøy.

1975 5 Mar. Vivian Beaumont Theatre, New York. Dir. Tormod Skagestad. N Liv Ullmann, H Sam Waterston.

1976 Renaissance-Theater, Berlin. Tr. and dir. Rudolf Noelte. Sc. Jürgen Rose. N Cordula Trantow, H Werner Kreindl.

1978 Haiyuza Theatre, Tokyo. Dir. Koreya Senda. N Kaneko Iwasaki, H Toru Takeuchi.

1978 27 Oct. City Theatre, Stockholm. Tr., adapt. and dir. Jan Håkanson. Sc. Akke Nordwall. N Lena Granhagen, H Leif Ahrle.

1981 30 Apr. Residenztheater, Munich. Tr. Heiner Gimmler. Adapt. and dir. Ingmar Bergman. Sc. Gunilla Palmstierna-Weiss. N Rita Russek, H Robert Atzorn.

1981 6 July. The Other Place, Stratford. Tr. Michael Meyer. Dir. Adrian Noble. Sc. Kit Surrey. N Cheryl Campbell, H Stephen Moore.

1981 Calgary. Dir. Richard Hornby.

1985 11 Oct. City Theatre, Gothenburg. Tr. Ernst Schönaich.
      Dir. Anu Saari. Sc. Elisabeth Åström. N Mariann Rudberg,
      H Jan Koldenius.

1988 12 Sept. Riverside Studio 1, London. Tr. Christopher
      Hampton. Dir. Jan Sargent. Sc. Stephanie Howard.
      N Anna Carteret, H Eamon Boland.

1989 17 Nov. Royal Dramatic Theatre, Stockholm. Tr. Klas
      Östergren. Adapt. and dir. Ingmar Bergman. Sc. Gunilla
      Palmstierna-Weiss. N Pernilla Östergren, H Per Mattsson.

1990 27 Oct. National Theatre, Oslo. Dir. Svein Sturla Hungnes.
      Sc. Lubos Hruza. N Gisken Armand, H Bjørn Skagestad.

1992 Jan. The Duke of Cambridge, London. Tr. Michael Meyer.
      Dir. Polly Irvin. Sc. Gabrielle Sabran. N Sophie Thursfield,
      H Timothy Bentinck.

RADIO

1937 23 July. Swedish Radio. Dir. Ernst Eklund.

1939 8 Dec. BBC. Tr. William Archer. Dir. Barbara Burnham.

1944 14 Dec. Swedish Radio. Dir. Ernst Eklund.

1947 12 May. BBC. Tr. William Archer. Dir. Howard Rose.
      N Vivienne Bennett, H Olaf Pooley.

1947 4 Dec. Swedish Radio. Dir. Alf Sjöberg. N Inga Tidblad,
      H Ulf Palme.

1950 15 Jan. BBC. Tr. and dir. Peter Watts. N Dulcie Gray,
      H Michael Denison.

1951 24 Jan. BBC. Tr. and dir. Peter Watts. N Marjorie
      Westbury, H Peter Coke.

1953 29 Jan. Swedish Radio. Dir. Lars-Levi Læstadius.
      N Gertrud Fridh, H Nils Fritz.

1959 3 July. BBC. Tr. William Archer. Dir. Frederick Bradnum.
      N Jill Bennett, H Jack May.

1965   23 May. BBC. Tr. Max Faber. Adapt. Charles Lefeaux.
1971   Norwegian Radio. Dir. Hans Heiberg. N Liv Ullmann,
        H Toralv Maurstad.
1986   12/19 Jan. Dutch Radio, TROS. Tr. and adapt. Nelly Nagel.
        Dir. Bert Dijkstra. N Teuntje de Klerk, H Paul van der Lek.

TELEVISION

1952   4 Nov. BBC. Tr. William Archer. N Joan Greenwood,
        H Hugh Burden.
1956   24 May. Tr. and adapt. Max Faber. N Mai Zetterling,
        H Griffith Jones.
1958   21 Dec. Swedish TV. Dir. Åke Falck.
1959   U.S. N Julie Harris.
1961   *Nora.* Bayerische Rundfunk. Adapt. and dir. Michael
        Kehlmann. Sc. Wolfgang Hundhammer. N Elfriede
        Kuzmany, H Paul Dahlke.
1970   17 Jan. Yorkshire Television. Tr. James McFarlane. Dir. Joan
        Kemp Welch. Sc. Natasha Kroll. N Anna Massey.
1970   27 Dec. *Ett dockhem.* Swedish TV. Adapt. and dir. Per
        Sjöstrand. Sc. Bibi Lindström. N Solveig Ternström,
        H Olof Bergström.
1973   *Nora oder Ein Puppenheim.* Schauspiel Frankfurt. Tr. Georg
        Schulte-Frohlinde. Dir. Hans Neuenfels. Sc. Klaus Gelhaar.
        N Elisabeth Trissenaar, H Peter Roggisch.
1974   14 Apr. Danish TV. Adapt. Leif Panduro. Dir. Palle
        Kjærulff-Schmidt. N Ghita Nørby, H Preben Neergaard.
1974   19 Apr. Norwegian TV in cooperation with Swedish TV.
        Dir. Arild Brinchmann. Sc. Christian Egemar. N Lise
        Fjeldstad, H Knut Risan.
1976   *Nora Helmer.* Saarländische Rundfunk. Adapt. and dir.
        Rainer Werner Fassbinder. Sc. Friedhelm Boehm. N Margit
        Carstensen, H Joachim Hansen.

1991   BBC. Tr. Joan Tindale. Dir. David Thacker. Sc. Marjorie
        Pratt. N Juliet Stevenson, H Trevor Eve.

FILM

1911   U.S. Thanhouser. Black-and-white, silent.
1915   U.S. Black-and-white, silent. Dir. Allan Holubar.
        N Dorothy Philips.
1917   U.S. Bluebird photoplay. Black-and-white, silent. Dir.
        Joseph De Grasse. N Dorothy Phillips, H William Stowell.
1917   *Ee Zertva* [Her Sacrifice]. Russia. Tovariscestvo. Black-and-
        white, silent. Dir. Ceslav Sabinskij. N Olga Gzovskaja,
        H Vladimir Gajdarov.
1918   U.S. Artcraft Photoplay. Black-and-white, silent. Dir.
        Maurice Tourneur. N Elsie Ferguson, H Holmes E. Herbert.
1922   U.S. Nazimova Productions. Black-and-white, silent.
        Adapt. Peter M. Winters. Dir. Charles Bryant. N Alla
        Nazimova, H Alan Hale.
1922   Germany. Projektions-AG Union. Black-and-white, silent.
        Adapt. Georg Fröschel/Berthold Viertel. Dir. Berthold
        Viertel. N Olga Tschechowa, H Carl Ebert.
1943   *Nora.* Argentina. Black-and-white. Dir. Ernesto Aranciba.
        N Delia Garcés, H Georges Rigaud.
1944   *Nora.* Germany. Ufa. Black-and-white. Adapt. Harald
        Braun and Jacob Geis. Dir. Harald Braun. N Luise Ullrich,
        H Viktor Staal.
1973   England. Elkins Productions/Freeward Films. Eastman
        colour, widescreen. Tr. Michael Meyer. Adapt. Christopher
        Hampton. Dir. Patrick Garland. N Claire Bloom,
        H Anthony Hopkins.
1973   England/France. World Film Services / Les Films la Boétie.
        Eastman colour, widescreen. Tr. Michael Meyer. Adapt.
        David Mercer. Dir. Joseph Losey. N Jane Fonda, H David
        Warner.

NOTES

PROLOGUE: BACKGROUND

1 'Notes for the Tragedy of Modern Times', quoted from *The Oxford Ibsen*, ed. James W. McFarlane, V, London, 1961, p. 436.

2 The background of the play is extensively described in Einar Østvedt's book-length study *Et Dukkehjem: Forspillet, Skuespillet, Efterspillet*, Skien, 1976.

3 Letter to Sophie Adlersparre, 24 June 1882, quoted from James W. McFarlane, ed., *Henrik Ibsen: A Critical Anthology*, Harmondsworth, 1970, p. 95.

4 Michael Meyer, *Henrik Ibsen*, II, London, 1971, p. 252.

5 Halvdan Koht, *Life of Ibsen*, tr. Einar Haugen and A.E. Santaniello, New York, 1971, p. 315.

6 *Ibid.*, p. 313.

7 *Ibid.*, pp. 311–12.

8 Elias Bredsdorff, *Den store nordiske krig om seksualmoralen*, Copenhagen, 1973, p. 7.

9 For a recent discussion of the matter, see Gail Finney, 'Ibsen and Feminism', in *The Cambridge Companion to Ibsen*, ed. James McFarlane, Cambridge, 1994, pp. 89–105.

10 Koht, *Life of Ibsen*, p. 317.

11 Michael Meyer, *Henrik Ibsen*, III, London, 1971, p. 297. – Ibsen actually said: '. . . to solve the woman question'.

12 Joan Templeton, 'The *Doll House* Backlash: Criticism, Feminism, and Ibsen', *PMLA*, 104:1, Jan. 1989, pp. 28–40.

13 Sandra Saari, 'Female Become Human: Nora Transformed', *Contemporary Approaches to Ibsen*, VI, Oslo, 1988, pp. 41–55.

14 Quoted from *The Oxford Ibsen*, V, pp. 436–7.

15 P. F. D. Tennant, *Ibsen's Dramatic Technique*, New York (1948), 1965, pp. 26–7.

16 Bergliot Ibsen, *De Tre*, Oslo, 1949, p. 186.

17 Letter 22 May 1879, quoted from *The Oxford Ibsen*, V, p. 435.

18 *The Oxford Ibsen*, V, p. 436.

19 *Ibid.*

20 John Northam, *Ibsen's Dramatic Method: A Study of the Prose Dramas*, London, 1953, pp. 33–4.

21 Thomas Bredsdorff, 'Byggesten til et dukkehjem', in Henrik Ibsen, *Et dukkehjem*, Copenhagen, 1985, p. 33.

22 Quoted from Michael Meyer's Introduction to Henrik Ibsen, *Plays: Two*, London, 1985, p. 19.

THE DRAMA TEXT

1 Tzvetan Todorov, 'The Two Principles of Narrative', *Diacritics*, I:1, Autumn 1971, p. 39.

2 For a discussion of the terms and a listing of the items belonging to the secondary text, see Egil Törnqvist, *Transposing Drama: Studies in Representation*, London, 1991, pp. 9–11.

3 Cf. Frederick J. and Lise-Lone Marker, *Ibsen's Lively Art: A Performance Study of the Major Plays*, Cambridge, 1989, p. 52.

4 Peter Reynolds, *Drama: Text into Performance*, Harmondsworth, 1986, p. 78.

5 Brian W. Downs, *A Study of Six Plays by Ibsen*, Cambridge, 1950, p. 112.

6 Cf. *The Oxford Ibsen*, V, p. viii.

7 Austin E. Quigley, *The Modern Stage and other Works*, New York, 1985, p. 93.

8 The dramaturgic sequence should not be confused with the cinematic one, which represents a section of a film taking place in one and the same time and space, what in Anglo-Saxon dramaturgy is referred to as 'scene'. A normal feature-length film will consist of no more than between five and forty sequences. See David Bordwell

and Kristin Thompson, *Film Art: An Introduction*, 4th edn, New York, 1993, pp. 63, 496.

9 Hermann J. Weigand, *The Modern Ibsen: A Reconsideration*, New York (1925), 1960, p. 41.

10 Northam, *Ibsen's Dramatic Method*, p. 16.

11 *Ibid.*, p. 16.

12 Jan Kott, *The Theater of Essence and Other Essays*, Evanston, Ill., 1984, p. 32.

13 Cf. Northam, *Ibsen's Dramatic Method*, pp. 26–31.

14 Yves Chevrel, *Henrik Ibsen: Maison de poupée*, Paris, 1989, pp. 60–2.

15 Jørgen Haugan, 'Trøfler, champagne og silkestrømper', in Lisbet Holst *et al.* (eds.), *Frigørelse: humaniora, digtning og sprog*, Kongerslev, 1981, p. 91.

16 Else Høst, 'Nora', *Edda*, 46, Oslo, 1947, p. 21.

17 Eric Bentley, *In Search of Theater*, New York, 1953, p. 350.

18 Northam, *Ibsen's Dramatic Method*, p. 19.

19 Brian Johnston, *Text and Supertext in Ibsen's Drama*, Pennsylvania State University Press, 1989, p. 145.

20 Quigley, *The Modern Stage*, pp. 99–100.

21 Richard Hornby, *Patterns in Ibsen's Middle Plays*, London and Toronto, 1981, pp. 104–5.

22 Quigley, *The Modern Stage*, p. 107.

23 Letter 8 Sept. 1881 to Heinrich Laube, quoted from *The Oxford Ibsen*, V, p. 455.

24 Quigley, *The Modern Stage*, p. 91.

25 *Ibid.*, p. 100.

26 Hornby, *Patterns*, pp. 114–15.

27 *Aristotle's Theory of Poetry and Fine Art*, ed. S. H. Butcher, New York, 1951, p. 31.

28 *Illustreret Nyhedsblad* 20 and 27 Dec. 1857, quoted from Michael Meyer, *Henrik Ibsen*, I, London, 1967, p. 169.

29 Horst Bien, *Henrik Ibsens Realismus*, Berlin, 1970, p. 156.

30 Letter to the Danish paper *Nationaltidende*, published there on 20 Feb. 1880.

31 *The Oxford Ibsen*, V, pp. 287–8.

32 Letter to Erik af Edholm, 3 Jan. 1880, quoted from *Henrik Ibsen: Brev 1845–1905. Ny samling*, ed. Øyvind Anker, Oslo, 1979, p. 248.

33 Hornby, *Patterns*, p. 93.

34 To Ibsen himself this was a completely open question. In his letter to Erik af Edholm, 3 Jan. 1880, he describes Nora as 'a great grown-up child who must venture out into life to discover herself and thereby perhaps at some later stage become suited to bring up children – or maybe not; no one can be sure'.

35 Weigand, *The Modern Ibsen*, p. 68.

36 Bien, *Henrik Ibsens Realismus*, p. 155.

37 David Thomas, *Henrik Ibsen*, London, 1983, pp. 72–3.

38 Errol Durbach, *A Doll's House: Ibsen's Myth of Transformation*, Boston, 1991, p. 133.

39 Cary M. Mazer, 'Ibsen and the Well-Made Play', in Yvonne Shafer, ed., *Approaches to Teaching Ibsen's A Doll House*, New York, 1985, pp. 69–75.

40 As Weigand does in his influential *The Modern Ibsen*, pp. 26–75, passim.

41 George Steiner, *The Death of Tragedy*, London, 1961, p. 291.

42 Cleanth Brooks and Robert B. Heilman, *Understanding Drama*, New York, 1961, Glossary, p. 45.

43 John Northam, 'Ibsen's Search for the Hero', in Rolf Fjelde, ed., *Ibsen: A Collection of Critical Essays*, Englewood Cliffs, N. J. 1965, p. 108.

44 Raymond Williams, *Modern Tragedy*, London, 1966, p. 98.

TRANSLATING ET DUKKEHJEM

1 Einar Haugen, *Norwegian–English Dictionary*, Oslo and Madison, 1965, p. 20.

2 Quoted from the *The Oxford Ibsen*, V, p. 455.

3 *Six Plays by Henrik Ibsen*, New York, 1957.

4 Quoted from Thomas F. Van Laan, 'English Translations of *A Doll's House*', in Yvonne Shafer, ed., *Approaches to Teaching Ibsen's A Doll House*, New York, 1985, p. 6. – Ironically, Ibsen's statement is rather muddled. What he meant to say is obviously that the meaning of the source text is frequently misunderstood first by incompetent translators, then by the readers confronted with the misleading renderings of these translators.

5 Letter 2 Aug. 1883, quoted from Evert Sprinchorn, ed., *Ibsen: Letters and Speeches*, New York, 1964, pp. 221–2.

6 Michael Meyer in Henrik Ibsen, *Plays: Two*, tr. Michael Meyer, London (1965), 1980, p. 105.

7 Van Laan, 'English Translations', p. 7. – The fact that Van Laan does not include Peter Watt's translation, brought out in the Penguin series, seems to reflect his American origin.

8 Van Laan, 'English Translations', p. 16.

9 *The Oxford Ibsen*, V, tr. and ed. James W. McFarlane, London, 1961; Henrik Ibsen, *Plays: Two*, tr. Michael Meyer, London (1965), 1980; Henrik Ibsen, *'A Doll's House' and Other Plays*, tr. Peter Watts, Harmondsworth (1965), 1985; Henrik Ibsen, *The Complete Major Plays*, tr. Rolf Fjelde, New York, 1965.

10 Introduction to *Four Major Plays*, pp. xv–xxvi.

11 Errol Durbach, *A Doll's House*, pp. 27–8.

12 Einar Haugen, *Ibsen's Drama: Author to Audience*, Minneapolis, 1979, p. 103.

13 Letter to Erik af Edholm, 3 Jan. 1880.

14 Erik M. Christensen, 'En meningsanalyse av Henrik Ibsens *Et dukkehjem*', in Atle Kittang and Asbjørn Aarseth, eds., *Hermeneutikk og litteratur*, Oslo, 1979, p. 126.

15 Van Laan 'English Translations', p. 14.

16 Introduction to Henrik Ibsen, *Four Major Plays*, xxxiv.

17 Quoted from *The Oxford Ibsen*, V, p. 458.

'A DOLL'S HOUSE' AS STAGE PLAY

1 Although the present chapter owes much to the survey in Markers' *Ibsen's Lively Art,* pp.46–89, my organisation of the material differs from theirs.

2 I am indebted to Drs Rob van der Zalm for this information.

3 For the early reception of the book and the play, see Tom Lerdrup Hansen's anthology and commentary *Kampen omkring Nora,* Copenhagen, 1988.

4 Herman Bang, *Kritiske Studier,* Copenhagen, 1880, p. 220.

5 Liv Ullmann, *Changing,* tr. Liv Ullmann, Gerry Bothner, Erik Friis, New York, 1977, p. 200.

6 Robert A. Schanke, *Ibsen in America: A Century of Change,* Metuchen, N.J., 1988, p. 6.

7 Per Erik Wahlund in *Svenska Dagbladet,* 31 Mar. 1962.

8 Schanke, *Ibsen in America,* p. 15.

9 Marker, *Ibsen's Lively Art,* p. 77.

10 Bodil Österlund and Marianne Grøndal, *Nora – ett dockhem genom åren,* Malmö, 1984, p. 33.

11 Marker, *Ibsen's Lively Art,* p. 53.

12 In a letter to Charles Archer, Sept. 1883. Quoted from *Edda,* 31, pp. 455–6.

13 Michael Egan, ed., *Ibsen: The Critical Heritage,* London, 1972, p. 104.

14 William Archer in *Theatrical 'World' for 1894,* London, 1895. Quoted from Northam, p. 22, note.

15 Martin Nag, *Ibsen i russisk åndsliv,* Oslo, 1967, pp. 57–9. Quoted from Marker, *Ibsen's Lively Art,* p. 64.

16 *Teatr i iskusstvo/Theatre and Art,* 1906/52. Quoted from Marker, *Ibsen's Lively Art,* pp. 63–4.

17 Konstantin Rudnitsky, *Meyerhold the Director,* Ann Arbor, 1981, p. 288.

18 Kristian Elster, *Teater 1929–1939,* ed. Anton Rønneberg, Oslo, 1941, p. 56.

19 Frederik Schyberg, *Berlingske Tidende*, 6 Mar. 1936. Reprinted in his *Ti Aars Teater*, Copenhagen, 1939, pp. 132–5, 168.

20 Schyberg, *Ti Aars Teater*, pp. 168–9. Quoted from Marker, *Ibsen's Lively Art*, p. 70.

21 *The Evening Standard*, 4 Mar. 1936, and *The Sunday Times*, 8 Mar. 1936.

22 James Agate, *Red Letter Nights*, London, 1944, p. 61.

23 Marker, *Ibsen's Lively Art*, p. 83.

24 Per Erik Wahlund, *Svenska Dagbladet*, 31 Mar. 1962.

25 Nils Beyer, *Stockholms-Tidningen*, 31 Mar. 1962.

26 Jarl Donnér, *Sydsvenska Dagbladet*, 8 Oct. 1972.

27 John Peter in *The Sunday Times*, 26 Jan. 1992.

28 Marker, *Ibsen's Lively Art*, p. 76.

29 *Dagbladet*, 25 Jan. 1974.

30 Marker, *Ibsen's Lively Art*, p. 75.

31 Reynolds, *Drama*, p. 79.

32 Sverker Andréason in *Göteborgs-Posten*, 12 Oct. 1985.

33 Bernard F. Dukore, 'A *Doll House* a Century Later', *New England Theatre Journal*, II:1, 1991, p. 3.

34 Jytte Wiingaard, *Teatersemiotik*, Copenhagen, 1987, p. 155.

35 Marker, *Ibsen's Lively Art*, p. 71.

36 Jarl Donnér in *Sydsvenska Dagbladet*, 8 Oct. 1972.

37 'Nora Helmer off for the Antipodes', an interview with Janet Achurch, *Pall Mall Gazette*, 5 July 1889.

38 William Lyon Phelps, *The Twentieth Century Theatre*, New York, 1918, p. 126.

39 Theodore Kommisarjevskaya, *Myself and the Theatre*, New York, 1930, p. 67.

40 Marker, *Ibsen's Lively Art*, p. 50.

41 Ove Rode, 'Et Teater i Forfald', *Verdens Gang*, 18 Oct. 1882. Quoted from Marker, *Ibsen's Lively Art*, p. 56.

42 Maurice Baring, *The Puppet Show of Memory*, Boston, 1992, pp. 210–11.

43 Koht, *Life of Ibsen*, p. 322.

44 *Ibid.*

45 Axel Otto Normann, *Johanne Dybwad: Liv og kunst*, Oslo, 1937, p. 97.

46 Unsigned, *Stockholms-Tidningen*, 11 Jan. 1925.

47 Österlund/Grøndal, *Nora – ett dockhem genom åren*, p. 24.

48 Schanke, *Ibsen in America*, p. 114.

49 Åke Janzon in *Svenska Dagbladet*, 8 Oct. 1972.

50 Ove Rode, 'Et Teater i Forfald'. Quoted from Marker, *Ibsen's Lively Art*, pp. 55–6.

51 Gerhard Gran, *Henrik Ibsen: Liv og Verker*, II, Christiania, 1918, p. 94. Quoted from Downs, *A Study of Six Plays by Ibsen*, p. 130, note 5.

52 Marker, *Ibsen's Lively Art*, p. 58.

53 Phelps, *The Twentieth Century Theatre*, p. 126.

54 A. Brustejn, *Stranicy proslogo*, 2nd edn, Moscow, 1956, p. 112. Quoted from Marker, *Ibsen's Lively Art*, p. 63.

55 Alfred Polgar, *Brahms Ibsen*, Berlin, 1910, p. 6. Quoted from Marker, *Ibsen's Lively Art*, p. 57.

56 Koht, *Life of Ibsen*, pp. 319–20.

57 Marker, *Ibsen's Lively Art*, p. 71.

58 *Ibid.*, p. 69.

59 Per Erik Wahlund, *Svenska Dagbladet*, 31 Mar. 1962.

60 Schanke, *Ibsen in America*, pp. 146–7.

61 Ullmann, *Changing*, pp. 209–10.

62 Halvdan Koht, 'Innledning' in Henrik Ibsen, *Samlede Verker*, VIII, Oslo, 1933, p. 255.

63 Beverly F. Elliott, 'Nora's Doors: Three American Productions of Ibsen's *A Doll House*', *Text and Performance Quarterly*, Vol. II, No. 10, 1990, pp. 194–5.

64 Odd Eidem, *Verdens Gang*, 26 Jan. 1974.

65 Evert Sprinchorn, 'Ibsen and the Actors', in Errol Durbach, ed., *Ibsen and the Theatre: The Dramatist in Production*, New York, 1980, p. 121.

66 Thomas Bredsdorff, 'Byggesten til et dukkehjem', p. 36.

67 Quoted from Marker, *Ibsen's Lively Art*, p. 51.

68 *Ibid.*, p. 51.

69 Bang, *Kritiske Studier*, pp. 314–15.

70 *The Detroit News*, 6 April 1975.

71 Gunilla Bergsten, *Upsala Nya Tidning*, 30 Oct. 1978.

72 Dan Sjögren, *Provinstidningen Dalsland*, 31 Oct. 1985.

73 Unsigned, *Idag*, 25 Jan. 1974.

74 Hornby, *Patterns*, p. 117.

75 Allan Fagerström, *Aftonbladet*, 8 October 1972.

76 Aud Thagaard, *Dagbladet*, 25 Jan. 1974.

77 William Archer, *The Theatrical 'World' for 1893*, London, 1894,
   p. 158.

78 *The New York Times*, 3 Mar. 1908.

79 Koht, *Life of Ibsen*, p. 323.

80 Ullmann, *Changing*, p. 210.

81 J. L. Bryan, 'The Opening Moments of *A Doll's House*: For
   Performance and Analysis in Class', in Yvonne Shafer, ed.,
   Approaches to Teaching Ibsen's A Doll House, New York, 1985, p. 94.

82 *Arbeiderbladet*, 14 Oct. 1936.

83 Schanke, *Ibsen in America*, p. 113.

84 Marker, *Ibsen's Lively Art*, p. 49.

85 Gran, *Henrik Ibsen*, II, p. 94.

86 Archer, *The Theatrical 'World' for 1893*, pp. 158–9. Quoted from
   Marker, *Ibsen's Lively Art*, p. 56.

87 Schanke, *Ibsen in America*, p. 15.

88 *The New York Sun*, 3 May 1905.

89 Edward Braun, *Meyerhold on Theatre*, New York, 1969, p. 25.

90 Kristian Elster in *Nationen*, n.d.

91 Hans Axel Holm, *Dagens Nyheter*, 19 May 1979.

92 Daniel Haakonsen, *Henrik Ibsen: Mennesket og Kunstneren*, Oslo,
   1981, p. 190.

93 Schanke, *Ibsen in America*, p. 9.

94 Herman Bang, *Masker og Mennesker*, Copenhagen, 1910,
   pp. 176–7. Quoted from Marker, *Ibsen's Lively Art*, p. 61.

95 Fr.v.d.L., *Morgenposten*, n.d.

96 *Göteborgs Handels- och Sjöfarts Tidning*, 9 Oct. 1972.

97 Ullmann, *Changing*, pp. 209–10.

98 *Politiken*, 25 Jan. 1974.

99 Ullmann, *Changing*, pp. 199–200.

100 Koht, *Life of Ibsen*, p. 322.

101 S. S-n., *Stockholms Dagblad*, 11 Jan. 1925.

102 Marker, *Ibsen's Lively Art*, p. 59.

103 *Ibid.*, p. 61.

104 Ullmann, *Changing*, p. 208.

105 Cf. Peter Iden in 'Über Ibsen's "Nora", Neuenfels und über Theaterkritik – am Beispiel von Theaterkritiken', *Theater Heute*, 1972, p. 35.

106 Gisela Ullrich in 'Über Ibsen's "Nora"', p. 37.

107 The German script has been published in English translation in Frederick J. and Lise-Lone Marker, *Ingmar Bergman: A Project for the Theatre*, New York, 1983, pp. 47–99. The book also contains a lengthy discussion of the production, pp. 19–31.

108 Marker, *Ingmar Bergman*, p. 23.

109 *Ibid.*, p. 20.

110 *Expressen*, 18 Nov. 1989.

111 The new technique used to create this background is known as Scanaprint.

112 August Strindberg, *Samlade Verk*, 16, ed. Ulf Boëthius, Stockholm, 1982, p. 14.

113 Bergman was not the first director who set the ending of the play in the marital bedroom. In his 1953 production Peter Ashmore did just that.

114 *Dagens Nyheter*, 18 Nov. 1989.

115 Chevrel, *Henrik Ibsen*, p. 108.

116 Cf. Bergman's film *Wild Strawberries* where three generations, born out of cold wombs, are fatefully linked to each other.

'A DOLL'S HOUSE' AS RADIO DRAMA

1 This is also true of television versions. Cf. Donald Wilson's observation that 265 dramatic works transmitted by BBC television would range in length from half an hour to ninety minutes. See George W. Brandt, ed., *British Television Drama*, Cambridge, 1981, p. 16.

2 Martin Esslin, *Mediations: Essays on Brecht, Beckett and the Media*, London, 1980, p. 183.

3 William Ash, *The Way to Write Radio Drama*, London, 1985, p. 43.

4 Bjørn Hemmer, 'Ibsen and the Crisis of Individual Freedom: Nora Helmer versus Rebekka Gamvik', in Bjørn Hemmer and Vigdis Ystad (eds.), *Contemporary Approaches to Ibsen*, VII, Oslo, 1991, p. 176.

'A DOLL'S HOUSE' AS TELEPLAY

1 For the distinction between 'hot' and 'cold' media, see Marshall McLuhan, *Understanding Media*, London, 1964, pp. 22 ff.

2 Cf. Heinz Schwitzke, 'Das Wort und die Bilder', in Irmela Schneider, ed., *Dramaturgie des Fernsehspiels*, Munich, 1980, p. 124.

3 Cf. Werner and Rose Waldmann, *Einführung in die Analyse von Fernsehspielen*, Tübingen, 1980, p. 110.

4 Leif Longum, 'Ibsen på TV-skjermen – en ny Ibsen?', in Harald Noreng (ed.) *En ny Ibsen?: Ni Ibsen-artikler*, Oslo, 1979, p. 126.

5 Seymour Chatman, *Story and Discourse: Narrative Structure in Fiction and Film*, Ithaca and London, 1978, pp. 194–5.

6 Quoted and translated from Gunnar Hallingberg, *Radio och TV-dramatik*, Lund, 1973, p. 172.

7 Birgitta Steene, 'Film as Theater: Geissendörfer's *The Wild Duck* (1976) from the Play by Henrik Ibsen', in Andrew S. Horton and Joan Magretta, eds., *Modern European Filmmakers and the Art of Adaptation*, New York, 1981, p. 297.

8 Quoted from Th. Borup Jensen, *Indføring i dramalæsning, TV hørespil*, Copenhagen, 1982, p. 49.

9 Henrik Brøndsted, 'Et Dukkehjem – Tv-teatret 1974', in *Den levende Ibsen: Analyser af udvalgte Ibsen-forestillinger 1973–78*, eds. Ulla Strømberg and Jytte Wiingaard, Copenhagen, 1978, p. 99.

10 Ronald Hayman, *Fassbinder: Film Maker*, New York, 1984, p. 144.

11 Jan Hogne Sandven in *Fem gange Et Dukkehjem*, Oslo, 1991, p. 18.

12 C. Braad Thomsen, '*Et Dukkehjem*. R. W. Fassbinder: *Nora Helmer*', in Ulla Strømberg and Jytte Wiingaard, eds., *Den levende Ibsen: Analyser af udvalgte Ibsen-forestillinger 1973–78*, Copenhagen, 1978, p. 82.

'A DOLL'S HOUSE' AS FILM

1 Michaela Giesing, *Ibsens Nora und die wahre Emanzipation der Frau*, Frankfurt, 1984, p. 6.

2 Schanke, *Ibsen in America*, p. 70.

3 André Bazin, 'Theater and Cinema', in *What is Cinema?*, I, tr. Hugh Gray, Berkeley, 1967, p. 90.

4 Foster Hirsch, *Joseph Losey*, Boston, 1980, p. 200.

5 *Ibid.*, pp. 202–3.

TRANSPOSING THE END OF 'A DOLL'S HOUSE'

1 Tadeusz Kowzan, 'The Sign in the Theater', *Diogenes*, 61, 1968, p. 73.

2 Erika Fischer-Lichte, *The Semiotics of Theater*, tr. Jeremy Gaines and Doris L. Jones, Bloomington and Indianapolis, 1992, p. 15.

3 Martin Esslin, *The Field of Drama: How the Signs of Drama Create Meaning on Stage and Screen*, London, 1987, pp. 103–5.

4 For a discussion of segmentation based on topical shifts, see Egil Törnqvist, *Strindbergian Drama: Themes and Structure*, Stockholm and Atlantic Highlands, N.J., 1982, pp. 22–32 and 119–46.

terms are borrowed from Bernard Beckerman, *Dynamics of Theory and Method of Analysis*, New York, 1970, p. 36.

6 This is my own rendering, closer to the original than that of the four translators.

7 Esslin, *The Field of Drama*, p. 9.

8 George W. Brandt, ed., Introduction to *British Television Drama*, Cambridge, 1981, p. 32.

9 Patrice Pavis, *Languages of the Stage: Essays in the Semiology of Theatre*, tr. Susan Melrose *et al.*, New York, 1982, p. 123.

EPILOGUE: IMPACT

1 Meyer, *Henrik Ibsen*, II, p. 454.

2 Koht, *Life of Ibsen*, p. 320.

3 Cf. Ian Britain, 'A Transplanted Doll's House: Ibsenism, Feminism and Socialism in Late-Victorian and Edwardian England', in *Transformations in Modern European Drama*, ed. Ian Donaldson, London, 1983, p. 32.

4 Koht, *Life of Ibsen*, p. 321.

5 Elisabeth Eide, 'Huaju Performances of Ibsen in China', *Acta Orientalia*, 44, 1983, pp. 100, 106.

6 Quoted from *The Oxford Ibsen*, V, p. 463.

7 From Harley Granville-Barker, 'The Coming of Ibsen', in *The Eighteen Eighties: Essays by Fellows of the Royal Society of Literature*, ed. by Walter de la Mare, Cambridge, 1930, as quoted in *The Oxford Ibsen*, V, pp. 459–60.

8 Published in *The English Illustrated Magazine*, Jan. 1890, pp. 315–25.

9 Britain, 'A Transplanted Doll's House', p. 24.

10 Giesing, *Ibsens Nora*, p. 2.

11 In *Images of Women in Literature*, ed. Mary Anne Ferguson, Boston, 1973, pp. 358–69.

12 Durbach, *A Doll's House*, pp. 131–2.

13 Giesing, *Ibsens Nora*, p. 2.

14 *Ibid.*, p. 3. An English version of Jelinek's play (by Tinch Minter) has been published in *Plays by Women*, 10, ed. Annie Castledir London, 1994.

15 Published in 1982 by Det Norske Samlaget, Oslo.

16 Ulf Boëthius, *Strindberg och kvinnofrågan till och med Giftas I*, Stockholm, 1969, pp. 258–9.

17 Cf. Martin Lamm, *Strindbergs dramer*, I, Stockholm, 1924, p. 260.

18 J.L. Wisenthal, ed., *Shaw and Ibsen*, Toronto, 1979, p. 49.

19 Bernard Shaw, *The Quintessence of Ibsenism* (1913), in *Major Critical Essays*, London, 1955, pp. 135, 138.

20 Letter to the *Evening Standard* (London), 30 November 1944. Quoted from Bernard F. Dukore, *Bernard Shaw: Playwright*, Columbia, Missouri, 1973, p. 54.

21 Wisenthal, *Shaw and Ibsen*, p. 61.

22 Bernard F. Dukore, *Bernard Shaw*, p. 60.

23 Jan Setterquist, *Ibsen and the Beginnings of Anglo-Irish Drama*, II, Uppsala, 1960, p. 94.

24 Lawrence Langner, *The Magic Curtain*, London, 1952, p. 288.

25 Doris Alexander, *The Tempering of Eugene O'Neill*, New York, 1962, p. 128.

26 Eugene O'Neill, *Thirst and Other One Act Plays*, Boston, 1914, p. 142.

27 *Ibid.*, p. 166.

28 Doris Falk, *Eugene O'Neill and the Tragic Tension: An Interpretive Study of the Plays*, New Brunswick, 1958, p. 15.

29 *Lost Plays of Eugene O'Neill*, New York, 1950, p. 84.

30 *Ibid.*, pp. 81–2.

31 Leif Longum, 'In the Shadow of Ibsen: his Influence on Norwegian Drama and on Literary Attitudes', in Anne Paolucci, ed., *Review of National Literatures: Norway*, 12, special ed. Sverre Lyngstad, New York, 1983, p. 86.

32 Peter Cowie, *Ingmar Bergman: A Critical Biography*, 2nd edn, London, 1992, p. 66.

ur Screenplays of Ingmar Bergman, tr. Lars Malmström and David ⁀ner, New York, 1960, p. 9.

usted version of Alan Blair's rather free translation in Ingmar *The Marriage Scenarios*, London, 1989, p. 2.

35 My adjustment of the rather free rendering in Bergman, *The Marriage Scenarios*, p. 6.

36 *Ibid.*, p. 65.

37 Ingmar Bergman, *Autumn Sonata*, tr. Alan Blair, New York, 1978, p. 5.

38 *Ibid.*, p. 49.

39 Letter to Gustaf af Geijerstam, 4 Jan. 1887. Quoted from *August Strindbergs Brev*, VI, Stockholm, 1958, p. 137.

40 *The Quintessence of Ibsenism*, p. 148.

SELECT BIBLIOGRAPHY

References to reviews, articles and fictional works other than *A Doll's House* are found only in the Notes.

PRIMARY WORKS

Ibsen, Henrik, *Et Dukkehjem*, Copenhagen, 1879
　　Ibsen's Prose Dramas, tr. and ed. William Archer, I, London, 1890
　　The Prose Dramas of Henrik Ibsen, ed. Edmund Gosse, tr. William
　　　Archer, I, New York, 1890
　　The Collected Works of Henrik Ibsen, tr. and ed. William Archer,
　　　VII, London, rev. edn, 1907
　　Samlede Verker: Hundreårsutgave, eds. Francis Bull, Halvdan
　　　Koht, and Didrik Arup Seip, VIII (includes *Et Dukkehjem*),
　　　Oslo, 1933, and XVII (*Brev 1872–1883*), Oslo, 1946
　　Six Plays by Henrik Ibsen, tr. Eva Le Galienne, New York, 1957
　　The Oxford Ibsen, ed. James W. McFarlane, V, tr. James W.
　　　McFarlane, London, 1961
　　Plays: Two, tr. Michael Meyer, London, 1965
　　A Doll's House and Other Plays, tr. Peter Watts, Harmondsworth,
　　　1965
　　Four Major Plays, I, tr. Rolf Fjelde, New York, 1965
　　Ibsen: Letters and Speeches, ed. Evert Spinchorn, New York, 1965
　　Henrik Ibsen: Brev 1845–1905. Ny samling, ed. Øyvind Anker,
　　　Oslo, 1979
　　Et dukkehjem, introd. and tr. Thomas Bredsdorff, Copenhagen,
　　　1985

SECONDARY WORKS

Agate, James, *Red Letter Nights*, London, 1944

Alexander, Doris, *The Tempering of Eugene O'Neill*, New York, 1962

Archer, William, *The Theatrical 'World' for 1893*, London, 1894
  The Theatrical 'World' for 1894, London, 1894

Ash, William, *The Way to Write Radio Drama*, London, 1985

Bang, Herman *Kritiske Studier*, Copenhagen, 1880

Baring, Maurice, *The Puppet Show of Memory*, Boston, 1922

Bazin, André, *What is Cinema?*, I–II, tr. Hugh Gray, Berkeley, 1967

Beckerman, Bernard, *Dynamics of Drama: Theory and Method of Analysis*, New York, 1970

Bien, Horst, *Henrik Ibsens Realismus*, Berlin, 1970

Boëthius, Ulf, *Strindberg och kvinnofrågan till och med Giftas I*, Stockholm, 1969

Bordwell, David and Kristin Thompson, *Film Art: An Introduction*, 4th rev. edn, New York, 1993

Brandt, George W., ed., *British Television Drama*, Cambridge, 1981

Braun, Edward, *Meyerhold on Theatre*, New York, 1969

Bredsdorff, Elias, *Den store nordiske krig om seksualmoralen*, Copenhagen, 1973

Brooks, Cleanth and Robert B. Heilman, *Understanding Drama: Twelve Plays*, New York, 1961

Butcher, S.H., ed., *Aristotle's Theory of Poetry and Fine Art*, New York, 1951

Chatman, Seymour, *Story and Discourse: Narrative Structure in Fiction and Film*, Ithaca and London, 1978

Chevrel, Yves, *Henrik Ibsen: Maison de poupée*, Paris, 1989

Cowie, Peter, *Ingmar Bergman: A Critical Biography*, 2nd edn, London, 1992

De la Mare, Walter, ed., *The Eighteen Eighties*, Cambridge, 1930

Donaldson, Ian, ed., *Transformations in Modern European Drama*, London, 1983

Downs, Brian W., *A Study of Six Plays by Ibsen*, Cambridge, 1950

Dukore, Bernard F., *Bernard Shaw: Playwright*, Columbia, Missouri, 1973

Durbach, Errol, *A Doll's House: Ibsen's Myth of Transformation*, Boston, 1991

ed., *Ibsen and the Theatre: The Dramatist in Production*, London, 1980

Egan, Michael, ed., *Ibsen: The Critical Heritage*, London, 1972

Elster, Kristian, *Teater 1929–1939*, ed. Anton Rønneberg, Oslo, 1941

Esslin, Martin, *The Field of Drama: How the Signs of Drama Create Meaning on Stage and Screen*, London, 1987

Falk, Doris, *Eugene O'Neill and the Tragic Tension: An Interpretive Study of the Plays*, New Brunswick, 1958

Fischer-Lichte, Erika, *The Semiotics of Theater*, tr. Jeremy Gaines and Doris L. Jones, Bloomington and Indianapolis, 1992

Fjelde, Rolf, ed., *Ibsen: A Collection of Critical Essays*, Englewood Cliffs, N.J., 1965

Giesing, Michaela, *Ibsens Nora und die wahre Emanzipation der Frau*, Frankfurt, 1984

Gran, Gerhard, *Henrik Ibsen: Liv og Verker*, I–II, Christiania, 1918

Haakonsen, Daniel, *Henrik Ibsen: Mennesket og Kunstneren*, Oslo, 1981

Hallingberg, Gunnar, *Radio och TV-dramatik*, Lund, 1973

Hansen, Tom Lerdrup, *Kampen omkring Nora*, Copenhagen, 1988

Haugen, Einar, *Norwegian-English Dictionary*, Oslo and Madison, 1965

Ibsen's Drama: Author to Audience, Minneapolis, 1979

Hayman, Ronald, *Fassbinder: Film Maker*, New York, 1984

Hemmer, Bjørn and Vigdis Ystad, eds., *Contemporary Approaches to Ibsen*, VII, Oslo, 1991

Hirsch, Foster, *Joseph Losey*, Boston, 1980

Holst, Lisbet *et al.*, eds., *Frigørelse: humaniora, digtning og sprog*, Kongerslev, 1981

Hornby, Richard, *Patterns in Ibsen's Middle Plays*, London and
Toronto, 1981

Horton, Andrew S. and Joan Magretta, eds., *Modern European
Filmmakers and the Art of Adaptation*, New York, 1981

Ibsen, Bergliot, *De tre*, Oslo, 1949

Jensen, Th. Borup, *Indføring i dramalæsning, TV-spil, hørespil*,
Copenhagen, 1982

Johnston, Brian, *Text and Supertext in Ibsen's Drama*, Pennsylvania
State University Press, 1989

Kittang, Atle and Asbjørn Aarseth, eds., *Hermeneutikk og litteratur*,
Oslo, 1979

Koht, Halvdan, *Life of Ibsen*, tr. Einar Haugen and A. E.
Santaniello, New York, 1971

Kommisarjevskaya, Theodore, *Myself and the Theatre*, New York,
1930

Kott, Jan, *The Theater of Essence*, Evanston, Ill., 1984

Lamm, Martin, *Strindbergs dramer*, I, Stockholm, 1924

Langner, Lawrence, *The Magic Curtain*, London, 1952

Marker, Frederick J. and Lise-Lone, *Ingmar Bergman: A Project
for the Theatre*, New York, 1983

Ibsen's Lively Art: A Performance Study of the Major Plays,
Cambridge, 1989

McFarlane, James W., ed., *Henrik Ibsen: A Critical Anthology*,
Harmondsworth, 1970

ed., *The Cambridge Companion to Ibsen*, Cambridge, 1994

McLuhan, Marshall, *Understanding Media*, London, 1964

Meyer, Michael, *Henrik Ibsen*, I-III, London, 1967–71

Nag, Martin, *Ibsen i russisk åndsliv*, Oslo, 1967

Normann, Axel Otto, *Johanne Dybwad: Liv og kunst*, Oslo, 1937

Northam, John, *Ibsen's Dramatic Method*, London, 1953

Österlund, Bodil and Marianne Grøndal, *Nora – ett dockhem
genom åren*, Malmö, 1984

Østvedt, Einar, *Et Dukkehjem: Forspillet, Skuespillet, Efterspillet*,
Skien, 1976

Pavis, Patrice, *Languages of the Stage: Essays in the Semiology of the Theatre*, tr. Susan Melrose *et al.*, New York, 1982

Phelps, William Lyon, *The Twentieth Century Theatre*, New York, 1918

Polgar, Alfred, *Brahms Ibsen*, Berlin, 1910

Quigley, Austin E., *The Modern Stage and Other Worlds*, New York, 1985

Reynolds, Peter, *Drama: Text into Performance*, Harmondsworth, 1986

Rudnitsky, Konstantin, *Meyerhold the Director*, Ann Arbor, 1981

Sandven, Jan Hogne, *Fem ganger Et Dukkehjem*, Oslo, 1991

Schanke, Robert A., *Ibsen in America: A Century of Change*, Metuchen, N.J., 1988

Schneider, Irmela, ed., *Dramaturgie des Fernsehspiels*, Munich, 1980

Schyberg, Frederik, *Ti Aars Teater*, Copenhagen, 1939

Setterquist, Jan, *Ibsen and the Beginnings of Anglo-Irish Drama*, I–II, Uppsala, 1951/1960

Shafer, Yvonne, ed., *Approaches to Teaching Ibsen's A Doll House*, New York, 1985

Shaw, George Bernard, *The Quintessence of Ibsenism* (1891, 1913), in *Major Critical Essays*, London, 1955

Strømberg, Ulla and Jytte Wiingaard, eds., *Den levende Ibsen: Analyser af udvalgte Ibsen-forestillinger 1973–78*, Copenhagen, 1978

Tennant, P. F. D., *Ibsen's Dramatic Technique* (1948), New York, 1965

Thomas, David, *Henrik Ibsen*, Macmillan Modern Dramatists, London, 1983

Törnqvist, Egil, *Strindbergian Drama: Themes and Structure*, Stockholm and Atlantic Highlands, 1982

Transposing Drama: Studies in Representation, London, 1991

Ullmann, Liv, *Changing*, tr. Liv Ullmann, Gerry Bothner, Erik Friis, New York, 1977

Waldmann, Werner and Rose, *Einführung in die Analyse von Fernsehspielen*, Tübingen, 1980

Weigand, Hermann J., *The Modern Ibsen: A Reconsideration* (1925), New York, 1960

Wiingaard Jytte, *Teatersemiotik*, Copenhagen, 1987

Wisenthal, J.L., ed *Shaw and Ibsen*, Toronto, 1979

INDEX

202